DIVINE LIVING

Embrace Your True Self

Inspired Guidance for Living an Enlightened Life.

KIRSTIE LILITH

INCLUDES

channelled wisdom from the Ascended Masters and Goddesses.

authors
AND CO.

ISBN13 Paperback: 978-1-915771-51-3

Contents

Prologue 1
Introduction 3

Part One
SPIRITUAL AWAKENING

1. Spiritual Awakenings 13
2. Yeshua (Jesus) 16
3. My Spiritual Awakening 19

Part Two
TRUST

4. Trust 29
5. Kali 38
6. My Animal Journey 41
7. Journey with the Whales Begins! 48

Part Three
CONTROL & BOUNDARIES

8. Control 59
9. Nagwal 63
10. Letting Go of Control 66
11. Boundaries 71
12. Setting Boundaries 75

Part Four
HEALING

13. Healing 83
14. Quan Yin 92
15. Healing Journey with the Whales 95

Part Five
PLAYING SMALL

16. Playing Small 101
17. Lilith 104
18. Stop Playing Small 107

Part Six
FEAR

19. Fear 113
20. Isis 116
21. The Retreat Begins! 118
22. Vulnerability 123
23. Here's to Being Vulnerable! 126

Part Seven
SURRENDER

24. Surrender 137
25. Lord Maitreya 141
26. The Welcome Committee 143

Part Eight
JOY

27. Joy 149
28. Melchizedek 152
29. Mission Day 154

Part Nine
IT'S OKAY

30. It's Okay 163
31. Metatron 166
32. The Day I Was Not Okay 168

Part Ten

DIVINE UNION

33. Divine Union 175
34. Mary Magdalene 180
35. The Ultimate Balance 183

Part Eleven

CONCLUSION

36. Final Words 189
37. Closing by Nagwal 191
38. Glossary of Ascended Masters and Goddesses 193
39. About the Author 195

For my sister, Kerry. Always in my heart.

For Nagwal, for having faith in me even when I lost faith in myself.

PROLOGUE

Writing this book has been an incredible journey and it has been a privilege to share my knowledge on all aspects of Divine Living. It has also been a huge honour to channel the Ascended Masters and Goddesses who stepped forward to assist and share their wisdom.

I am passionate about fulfilling my soul's purpose to demonstrate an authentic way of living in perfect Divine union. To me, life is magical – it's not just about surviving; it's about thriving! To be able to live each day in joyful harmony with the universe is not just a pipe dream; it is attainable.

It is my hope that you also enjoy the sharing of my own personal experiences. Whether you consider parts of my story to be courageous, over dramatic, inspirational or sometimes just downright idiotic, I will leave that in your hands. To me, it has been an amazing adventure and I have had the opportunity and privilege of meeting some incredible people. What you take from this book will be individual to you all, as it is with every experience that we encounter throughout life. If I had just one wish, it would be that my story may inspire you on your own journey and to recognise that nothing is impossible. I consider myself an ordinary person who had the opportunity to achieve something extraordinary.

Introduction

What does it mean to live divinely?

It means living your life in flow with the universe; being able to live your life in complete harmony with absolute peace and joy. To feel connected to your inner light and to radiate that out into the world around you; to be able to live from the heart and choose to react from a place of love and not fear; to not sweat the small stuff and recognise that there is a higher purpose to life...That is what Divine Living means to me.

Is this achievable? Yes. Is this easy? Not always!

This book is a guide to living in connection with the Divine. This book will show you how you can learn to surrender more and have more faith and trust in yourself. It will demonstrate how you can start to let go of fear, let go of control and allow yourself to live more from the heart.

Aren't you tired of constantly feeling that you're not good enough? Have you had enough of feeling out of balance, feeling that life is a struggle? Feeling that you are constantly striving for something but not really sure what that is? Do you question that there must be more to life than this?

It is so tiring, moving through life when you just feel that it is a constant struggle, worrying about what might happen, what has happened and feeling that you have no control over any of it. It is exhausting. It is like trying to push water uphill – not easy and not very satisfying! Living in your head with a constant loop of worry, stress and fear is exhausting. Thinking that you're failing. Thinking that surely life must be easier than this.

Are you ready to step off that hamster wheel of life and embrace something new?

Let me share a secret with you. Divine Living is not just attainable by monks sitting and meditating in a temple all day. Divine Living is attainable by all of us. That includes you.

In life, we are given many learning opportunities and are introduced to various potential guides and teachers. It is important that, for each and every one of these encounters, you listen to your heart and follow what resonates with you and your journey. Allow yourself the possibility of absorbing a different perspective but always be true to yourself. I am a Divine channel. This means that I connect with and bring messages through from higher beings – Ascended Masters, Archangels and Goddesses to name a few. My journey with the Divine has given me many opportunities to experience what it means to live divinely. This has not always been easy. I have been pushed to my limits (and beyond) and put into situations that I could not even have dreamed of. A big part of my spiritual journey is to experience first-hand what it means to be in flow with the Divine. It is only through my own experiences that I can teach and share with others. Trialling what works and what doesn't work effectively enables me to guide others on their own journey. This does not mean to say that there is only one path and that my way is the only way. What is written in this book is based on my experiences, the knowledge gained on my path and information from Divine beings. It is not absolute; it is just my truth.

I hope what I have learnt will give you the confidence that Divine Living is achievable. It also allows you to go easy on yourself. It is not about getting it right the first time, it is about being willing to try. It is about being willing to keep on trying and to be open to new possibilities. I am also not declaring, by the way, that I have reached Ascended Master status! I am still walking my journey towards living in flow with the Divine in each and every moment. I achieve this state much more now than I ever did, but it is about recognising there is no perfection or final destination. It is a way of 'being'. What I do, however, is show up every single day and commit to this path.

Committing to this path will allow you a sense of freedom, a feeling that there is a higher purpose in life. When you make the decision to let go of control and fear and to live in joy and harmony, the things that would normally have bothered you seem to become more insignificant. As the saying goes, don't sweat the small stuff. It does not mean that life suddenly becomes all unicorns and rainbows. The ripples of life will still happen – good and bad – but there will be a greater sense of peace and calmness within you.

My life has changed beyond recognition. I surrender more to the flow of life and see experiences as opportunities rather than being triggered into a fear response. I am the happiest that I have ever been, and I wake every morning with a sense of peace and joy. It's that feeling of child-like excitement and wonder for what today will bring, an inner calmness and a grounding sense of knowing that regardless of what happens, I will be able to cope. My clients that I have mentored in living this way can see the positive changes in their lives too. They feel much more in control of themselves as they have begun to let go of trying to control external influences. They are aware of when they are triggered by life circumstances and go into a helpful self-inquiry rather than a hopeless spiral of emotions. This way of living has given them and me a deep sense of purpose and contentment.

If you, too, decide to follow the ideals and way of life shared in this book, your perspective on life will totally change. When you truly commit to being open to a new way of being and allow yourself to embrace these teachings, you will obtain a level of happiness and understanding that you would not have previously thought achievable.

I will be sharing how to live more in joy and happiness – not just fleeting moments when you're surprised with a bouquet of flowers, but a deep and permanent shift, where your entire essence grows from a place of joy. You will be able to let go of the desire to control external situations and recognise that you can only control your own energy.

This book will also take you through processes of how you can connect with your own spirit guides so that you can receive personal divine guidance. Each and every one of us has access to divine support, all we need to do is ask and learn how to receive the answers. A selection of Ascended Masters and Goddesses will also be offering their own words of wisdom throughout the book regarding the art of living divinely. These sections are completely channelled by them and offer invaluable insight into how to achieve an enlightened state.

We will go on a journey of learning the art of fully surrendering, allowing and trusting. Not just half-hoping that your job is secure or that you will have enough money, but wholly knowing in every cell of your body that you are protected and supported. This is something that nobody finds easy, but I can assure you that it is achievable. It just takes practice.

We will look at the pitfalls of fear and judgement and how they can cripple you into inaction, which does not support expansion or moving forward with your life. All of this empowers you to progress on your own healing journey as I share various methods of healing and clearing traumas both from your current life and past lives.

I will be sharing my own experiences as to how I have moved through the various stages of Divine Living. The aspects of healing, trusting, surrendering and letting go of control and fear. I will share how I have been pushed to my limit sometimes to really understand and embody living in flow with the universe. In particular, I will share insights into my recent journey with the humpback whales, which was life-changing in so many ways. But the main learning for me was having to surrender to my fears and doubts in ways that I had not even imagined. My journey with the whales will hopefully inspire you on your own path as you recognise that anything is possible if you just allow and fully let go. I like to lead by example and to use my life as a means to demonstrate a different way of living – a way of living by Divine will and being aligned with your own divinity.

Many religions and cultures have different ways of describing this state of 'being' or 'living'. Buddhism refers to this as Nirvana, the awakened state. More Western traditions refer to it as Christ Consciousness, ascension or enlightenment. Over the millennia, there have been many teachers and masters who have walked this earth – Buddha, Jesus and Babaji, to name just a few. They guide us in showing us the way to achieve this state of being. Different traditions describe this state using different words, but they all pertain to the same goal. No matter what route you take, the objective is the same: to reach that state where you can align with All That Is, source energy, creator energy, however you wish to define it. This is a state of living with open awareness, in love and non-judgement. To be able to see through these eyes of complete compassion is indeed Divine Living. Just know that your path will be individual to you, there is no right or wrong. Some may take a longer route; others will be more direct.

Whatever your route, it does not mean to say that it will be easier or harder than another. Our individual paths with the Divine are just that – individual. Some days, you will feel like giving up, like things don't seem to be working and like you aren't making any progress. But I assure you that there will also be days when you get breakthroughs, days when you will glimpse moments of living in perfect flow and days when you feel connected to yourself as never before and experience love and joy coursing through every cell in your body. THOSE days make it all worthwhile.

To connect to your divinity is simple. As mentioned before, this does not mean that it is always easy. We all tend to look outside of ourselves for the answers. We try to attain the awakened state by the thinking mind. The process can't be forced or made to happen. It can be achieved in many ways but ultimately, it is about an inner philosophy, practising a way of being with compassion and love. The insights that we gain from books and courses can provide valuable pointers to our own journey, however, ultimately the answer lies within ourselves. It is a case of remembering 'where' it is and 'how' to align with it. The solution is simple, the path to the solution, not so much!

Even though this path to a fully awakened state can be a lonely one at times and a path that only we, ourselves, can walk, luckily, the universe provides us with companions along the way. Along this spiritual path, we find ourselves connecting with people who are walking a similar path. Some may be at a similar level to us and can be someone to bounce ideas off and enable us to feel less alone. Others will be further along than us and able to provide us with the motivation and valuable insights that we need to keep moving forward. We may find ourselves being that person for someone else too, able to share our own inner wisdom to accelerate their journey.

To me, it is about following our inner compass, the inner guidance system that we all have, following the breadcrumbs of joy and compassion, allowing the Divine to lead us back home. This book is designed to show you how you can start living in this way, giving simple steps and insights that will support you to start or continue this path towards enlightenment. Living divinely can start NOW. It can start today, at this very moment.

You can make the decision to join me and to start living in harmony with the Divine, right here, right now. All you need to do is to decide and then just take a deep breath and surrender. Allow me to guide you on your next steps. We've got this.

PART ONE

SPIRITUAL AWAKENING

Chapter 1

Spiritual Awakenings

> *There will come a time when you believe everything is finished.*
>
> *That will be the beginning.*
>
> — *Louis L'Amour*

When people have what is referred to as a 'spiritual awakening', it can feel so dramatic, full-on and uncomfortable. The experience can sometimes be quite a distinctive end to the path that you were on and then a massive leap in a whole new direction. One client described her awakening as if she'd been walking around in a bubble of cotton wool and wearing sunglasses: She had been numb to fully feeling and experiencing what was around her and seeing life through a filtered lens. Once the awakening happened, the cotton was lifted, the glasses removed, and she could truly feel all of life; the silken touch of flower petals and the crisp bite of the wind. The sky was no longer 'pale', but vibrant in its colours. She was alive and feeling everything.

These spiritual awakenings are like a one-way trip – you can't go backwards. Once you have been shown that new perspective or are put on a completely different path, there is rarely a way to go back to the 'way things were' (sorry folks!). It is quite normal for there to be a lot of resistance and reluctance to move forward on this new path as it feels very scary and unknown. We sometimes stay with what we know, even if we intrinsically know that it isn't good for us because it's better to be with the devil, we know than let go and step into the unknown, regardless of whether this might open up greater opportunities. In my experience though, I have found that the Divine have infinite patience, and they are always right behind you, encouraging you to keep moving forward at every juncture when your natural instinct is to want to turn around and run back the way that you came!

I feel that these awakenings need to be dramatic as I don't think that we pick up or listen to the subtle suggestions that the Divine is patiently whispering in our ears. I feel that when the dramatic awakening or shift in direction occurs, we've actually missed the umpteen previous subtle signs! The Divine needs to give us quite a strong push to actually get our attention and to 'force' us onto this new path. Obviously, in the bigger scheme of life, there is no forcing. As souls, we have chosen this path that we are on – we just forget this when we incarnate into a physical body, so we require these shifts and nudges from the Divine. As with everything in our life we always have free will and can choose to ignore these nudges. We may not be able to shift our awareness back to our old way of thinking after an awakening, but we always have the option of just sitting down on our new path and refusing to budge! It may become uncomfortable, but we always have that free will!

As we become more adept at listening to the subtle signs, the need for these 'dramatic' changes is no longer required. At this point, we are more in tune with the Divine and the universe and life starts to make a little more sense. I also believe that these spiritual awakenings happen in perfect divine timing in accordance with our soul's path. Our soul has chosen at exactly what point in time it wishes to have a course corrected, so to speak. These timeframes are usually quite short, which results in the big or dramatic shifts that we experience. After this life path correction, there is usually less need for the intensity of further spiritual awakenings.

A lot of people have these spiritual awakenings and as with the whole of life, they are unique to the person experiencing them. It becomes part of their story, part of their individual journey. It can be helpful to hear about other people's experiences as it can assist you in processing and moving through your own awakening. Nobody's experiences, or awakenings, are better or worse than others, they are just part of the individual journey. The more that you can let go and surrender, the easier the awakenings are. I appreciate that this is not always possible. The surrendering only really comes when you have a greater awareness of what is happening. This may not be achievable with your current situation, so sometimes, the only way is to just get through each day. There may not be grace and flow in this and that's okay. Sometimes in life, just getting through each day is enough. This is not failing. It is surviving.

Chapter 2

Yeshua (Jesus)

My dearest brothers and sisters, it is my deepest pleasure to be able to converse with you and share my guidance and wisdom. This is a time I have been waiting for since I walked on Earth in a physical incarnation. When I was here on Earth, planting the seeds of the Christ Consciousness, it was in preparation for this moment. For this now. For the Earth, and you dear ones, to be ready to embody and awaken to your true natures. You all hold the Christ Consciousness within you. Your cells hold the DNA of Christ Consciousness. There is a memory deep within you that holds the blueprint for Divine Living, a blueprint in which you live in conjunction with your truest self, your highest self, in complete balance and harmony within yourself, between each other and also within the entire universe. It is when you live in this state that everything finally makes sense. This meaning and this sense of purpose provide peace and contentment from deep within. The capacity for love that you currently hold moves to a deeper level than you could even think possible.

My dear ones, I urge you to start following the teachings laid out in this book. Start your journey today. Allow yourself this opportunity to be fully awake during this lifetime. This state is completely achievable. It just requires a willingness and a desire from you to want this. In this moment, take a breath and commit to this path. Agree to step forward, hand in hand with me and allow me to walk with you as you embark on this journey, the journey back to your true self. Allow me to walk you home.

Some of you will find this path easier than others. This does not mean to say that some of you are doing it better than others. Some will find certain aspects easier than others. Some of you will find it easier to fully surrender, some may struggle with letting go of fear. Just know that all of this programming has been with you for millennia. It is all very familiar, so it is not always easy to say goodbye to. Treat yourself with infinite love and kindness. Try and see yourself through the eyes of the Divine, my eyes. Try and see yourself as the perfect being that you are, radiating and shining with the most beautiful and infinite light and love. This is how I see you, dear ones, because this is how you truly are. Now is the time for you to start awakening and remembering this fact.

Start each day anew. Allow yourself to absorb the meaning of the teachings and each day, start anew with fresh energy, with a fresh outlook. Treat yourself with the infinite love and gentleness that you would a babe trying to take its first uncertain steps in the world. Know that you will stumble along the way. Know that you will not achieve perfection. There is no perfection to attain, it is just an ideal. Do not perceive your journey as a series of 'wins' or 'failures'. Allow yourself to expand beyond these limitations. See your journey as just that – YOUR journey. One that is unique to you with all the perfect twists and turns. Allow yourself to see that bumps in the road are just part of your journey, part of your unique path. You are not doing it 'wrong'; it is just part of your story which is unfolding in perfect divine timing.

Allow me to be beside you as you take your first faltering steps. Allow me to help lift you back up when you stumble. I am with you always through this journey. I have complete faith in you, dear ones, that you have the ability and the courage to open yourself to remembering your true nature. Your divinity. Now is the time for you to all start living in this way. In love, in peace and in harmony. I radiate and surround you with my love and light as we choose to walk this path together. I welcome you home to yourself.

Chapter 3

My Spiritual Awakening

In order to fully appreciate my work with the Divine and the animals, it is necessary to have some insight into my life and my journey and how it evolved. None of us are 'born' into who we are today, it is a cycle of life events and circumstances that lead us to this point. I wish to share with you my own spiritual awakening.

I was born and raised in the UK and until 2014, I lived quite a conventional life. I went to university, got a corporate job, I was even married! You know, the usual and 'normal' lifestyle of conforming. In 2014, this all changed.

I had been under a lot of stress and pressure the previous year due to bereavement, work and the usual life pressures. My health started deteriorating without me really realising it. I withdrew into myself, instinctively trying to conserve whatever energy I had. I felt like a hollow shell, just going through the motions of my busy life. I started drinking too much alcohol and just focused on juggling my work and family life. Some days, I could hardly breathe and the pressure in my chest was so painful I thought my heart would explode out of my ribcage. I had no idea what was happening to me and no available energy to try and figure it out. My health continued to deteriorate until I finally had a mental breakdown in April 2014.

At this point, I thought that I had reached rock bottom, but I was wrong. I said to myself, at least nothing worse could happen to me. My hope was misplaced. The next day, my husband, without any warning or discussion, said he was leaving me. Blood drained from my face as he told me. The only sound that I could muster was 'oh,' as the little bit of energy I had left was ripped out of me. My marriage was over. The husband that I thought I would grow old with no longer loved me. My mind could not piece together these facts. I sank to the floor in a heap, too shell-shocked to even cry. I clutched my knees to my chest and rocked back and forth. Time lost all meaning. I had found my rock bottom.

I honestly don't know how I made it through the next few months. I was at the lowest point I had ever been in my life, and I didn't know how to continue living. It was a struggle to get through each day. Just getting out of bed some days was too much and a seemingly simple action like brushing my teeth was sometimes such a huge task. Coupled with the breakdown, I was also dealing with severe depression and anxiety. In addition, I now had to cope with and process the ending of my marriage. Those days were the darkest of my life. I contemplated suicide many times, as it seemed a more appealing option than to continue trying to get through each day. All I could see was darkness, any joy that I had felt had been eliminated and I struggled to see how things could get better. The pain of having my heart ripped out of my chest remained my constant companion. I felt like I was drowning in my emotions – shame, hurt, loneliness and despair – I had fallen into a huge pit and each day I clung on by my fingernails as I tried to claw my way back out.

Looking back, it was obvious, but at the time I was unaware of the fact that I was going through a spiritual awakening. I also had no idea until later, that the Goddess Kali had entered my life to open me up to my spiritual path. There is usually a lot of destruction and chaos involved when she chooses to work with you, and I can testify to that. As already mentioned, it was a very dark time in my life. My life as I knew it was destroyed and I struggled to get through each day. In the midst of all the rubble that used to be my life, I was given an opportunity to 'rise from the ashes' and to rebuild it with Kali's help.

It was at this point that I began my personal healing journey with the Goddess, and I entered the ever-evolving process of healing trauma from this life as well as past lives. It is not an easy path to walk and it takes a lot of courage to keep diving into those deep dark places that hold all our trauma. Sometimes though, we do not know what we are capable of until we have been through such darkness.

In order to fully process what you've been through, it's useful to take time to observe and look back on your journey. Sometimes it is so easy to skip this part and constantly focus on where you are going next. When you take the time to pause and look back on your path, you can start to see how the dots that relate to key significant life events join up, leading you to where you are at this very moment. Things that maybe didn't make sense at the time suddenly become much clearer as you realise their purpose or significance. It also allows you to appreciate and recognise what you are capable of and how strong you are. Sometimes, you need to be your own advocate in life and give yourself a well-deserved pat on the back.

Without this reflection time, all you can ever see is the next step in front of you because the next moment in time is your only guarantee in life, the present breath that takes you to the next breath. During my dark times, I could only see the dots of my past that took me to this pile of rubble that was now my life. I could not see where my life was heading, all I could see was darkness in front of me. It is not easy to sit in that space of darkness, not knowing how to proceed, but in spiritual awakenings, it is usually a necessity. I decided I had a choice to make – I either could stay where I was and continue to wallow in my ruined life, or I could keep walking and see where life took me. So, I took a deep breath and stepped forward.

One step at a time, blindly moving forward and learning to trust more and more, my Divine guidance took me along a path that led me to some amazing spiritual practitioners who lived near me. These people helped me to start to shift and release the emotional baggage I was carrying. I worked with an amazing shamanic practitioner for a few years who really helped me to progress along my journey. She helped me, for example, to accept my dysfunctional childhood and the ending of my marriage, as well as to release the fear of public emotions. I sometimes struggled with this process of healing in company as I am naturally an introverted person, so to allow my emotions out in public was difficult for me. I think we all find it hard to be vulnerable, especially around others. In a private setting with my shaman, it was easier to express the emotions I held inside, whereas, in a group setting, I would try and hold in my tears as I felt so embarrassed. Experience has taught me that trying to restrict the emotions from escaping is not a good plan, as they seem to have a mind of their own and they will escape at some point, typically a lot louder and more dramatically than if I had allowed them to flow naturally in the first instance. I remember one particular time, while on a day retreat, being hit by a tidal wave of emotion that I tried to suppress as I felt so embarrassed that I had already spent most of the day crying. In trying to suppress my tears, the noise that came out of my mouth sounded more like a cat being loudly strangled. I was mortified, as everyone naturally swivelled around to see where this noise was coming from. It would have been far less traumatic if I had just allowed my tears to fall naturally!

During this healing period, I was held in the loving and compassionate arms of the Goddesses, Mother Mary and Quan Yin. The patience these two Divine beings had was infinite and I have so much love and gratitude for them. I think I set a new world record for the amount of crying an individual can do. I often refer to myself as 'the well of endless tears'. These beautiful Divine beings held space for me and helped me move through my healing journey. There was probably not a lot of grace involved in my healing, but I still kept on showing up and putting one foot in front of the other.

Even though I was assisted during all this healing by practitioners, ultimately, it is a path that you can only take alone. Others can help give insights and facilitate your healing but ultimately it is your path, and no one can do the healing for you. To this day, a lot of my journey is spent alone, witnessing, releasing and allowing whatever needs to come up and be healed at the time. Sometimes, when I thought I could go no further, I found a new level of resilience that I didn't know I had, which kept me moving forward. When I healed so much from this life and started to think I was nearly complete, I quickly realised I had just reached the tip of the iceberg. It is then that past lives start to crawl out of the woodwork to be given the opportunity to be released. It was not an easy journey, but it was one I felt compelled at a really deep level to follow.

There is no requirement for anyone to undertake this deep personal healing. I often think that it is sometimes a path best avoided! It is a painful and difficult road and most definitely not for the fainthearted. I know that I make a conscious choice each and every day to continue moving along this path, but I feel it goes deeper than just a decision. It feels as if my soul has chosen this journey and that I came here in this incarnation to heal myself fully so that I can embrace the divinity within me again. I feel that many have chosen a similar path and that I am by no means alone. My purpose in this lifetime is to be a 'way show-er' and an 'ascension guide', although during my spiritual awakening, I was blissfully unaware of my soul purpose or what was in store for me. All I was doing was getting through each day, treading water, trying not to drown and praying that things would get easier!

My work with the Goddess Lilith was particularly transformational, deep and enlightening. She is a 'dark' Divine Feminine being. It is uncomfortable working with her as she opens you up to acknowledging your own inner 'darkness'. Her work with me was ultimately about accepting all parts of myself, the 'dark' and the 'light'. We typically want to see the good in ourselves and are sometimes willing to ignore the desires, the judgement and the anger that we also have. Lilith does not allow you this luxury. She gave me the opportunity, for example, to really face the anger that I suppressed within my body. I was so proficient at holding my anger in, I had no concept that I was doing this and just assumed I had no anger to express. I was wrong! I will forever be in awe of the journey that she took me on and how she changed my life and my perception of myself. This deep transformation is what led me to eventually take her name as my own a few years later.

My journey with the Goddess is ultimately about allowing the feminine energy within me to rise, to embrace that energy and to allow her to have a place once more in my life. There is a lot of talk these days about the rise of the feminine, the Goddess, the Divine Feminine. However we identify, we all have that divine spark within us, we are all connected to source energy, the infinite. To become aware of this fact and to be able to align with our divinity, we first need to find a balance within ourselves. Finding the balance between the masculine and the feminine energies within us has nothing to do with gender but is based on the qualities these energies bring forward. Once we are working in harmony with these energies, we can then look to embody the Divine Masculine and Divine Feminine within us. This is called Divine Union and will be discussed in further detail later in the book.

During my spiritual awakening years, I trained in various spiritual modalities; reiki, crystals, animal communication and mediumship to name a few. At the time, as mentioned previously, my path was not clear. I was just following the spiritual breadcrumbs and seeing where it led. Looking back, I can now see how all the training has woven itself perfectly to form the tapestry that is my current life. My training in mediumship, even though at times painful and difficult, has been the foundation for my work. It has given me confidence in my own ability to work with client's spirit guides, animals, ascended masters and the angelic and galactic realms, without the need for external validation.

Today, my life has completely transformed from what it was previously, and in 2019, I made the decision to dedicate my life to the Divine and to fulfil this purpose full-time. I resigned from my corporate job. Since making this decision, I have been able to expand my spiritual business and assist people and animals alike on their soul paths. These days, I have the pleasure of being an animal communicator, working with both domestic and wild animals. I love being able to give them a voice and to connect owners with their animals, past and present. I also have the pleasure of helping people on their journey by offering guidance, mentoring and retreats. I am truly blessed to be able to wake up every day doing something that fills me and others with so much joy.

Rewinding now and going back to my spiritual awakening days, I noticed that I started to get feelings in my stomach or a knowing when I had a decision to make. When I followed these signs, I quickly realised that life unfolded much easier than if I ignored the signs. My curiosity was piqued, and I started to follow my intuition and guidance more and more to see where it led. One such thread led me to meet an animal communicator. Following my gut instinct, I asked her to train me. She said yes.

Part Two

TRUST

Chapter 4

Trust

> *Trust dreams.*
>
> *Trust your heart,*
>
> *And trust your journey.*
>
> — *Neil Gaiman*

A big part of Divine Living is trust – trusting in our soul's journey and trusting that, at some level, we know the way. Trust in yourself, trust in spirit, trust in the Divine. Trusting in yourself is about trusting your feelings, your intuition and your gut instinct. Trusting in your spirit guides and the Divine is trusting in a plan bigger or greater than yourself. Know, trust and have faith that there is a greater plan unfolding which transpires in perfect divine timing. We all have free will, every single being on this planet has free will. But there is also divine will, where we can choose to surrender our own free will to follow the will of the Divine. Following divine will is understanding that there is a bigger plan at play, and we only get to see such a small part of it at any one time, whereas the Divine gets to see the whole tapestry and how everything and everyone weaves together perfectly. Following divine will and divine timing does not absolve you from making any decisions. Action is still required but it is inspired action rather than action for the sake of it. It is trusting in your guidance and knowing that there is a perfect timing for everything.

Trusting in the Divine means choosing to trust in something bigger than yourself. Trust your guidance in whatever way it shows up for you. Believe in something greater than yourself. Keep showing up every day, even though, a lot of the time, you may have no idea what you are doing or where it will lead. Our guidance can be so subtle, that it can be easy to miss. It can be very easy to ignore as guidance usually starts as a quiet whisper, an intuitive feeling, a gut reaction. Acting on that guidance takes trust, it takes faith. It is about having trust and faith in the Divine even when you feel you have lost trust and faith in yourself.

We all have a team of spirit guides who have chosen to be with us and help guide us through our lives. We do not have to have contact with them, they have signed up to help us no matter what, but how amazing would it be if we could build a relationship with them, listen to them, hear their guidance and choose to act on that guidance? How amazing to know that we are not in this on our own; we have a whole support team at our disposal just ready to offer guidance when needed. We have various types of guides that are on our team. Some are with us for our whole life and others are with us for certain aspects of it. The ones that are our guides for a certain length of time, I like to call them 'specialists' as they enter our life for a specific reason or purpose. It may be that we are undergoing training, r starting a family or having a spiritual awakening. There are various times in our life when having specialist help is advantageous, so specialist guides step in to help during these times and then move on to help others going through similar challenges when our need has been fulfilled.

Our guides can consist of loved ones (relatives that have passed back to spirit) or people that have previously incarnated on Earth (for example, Native American people, monks or priestesses). We can also have higher beings on our team such as angelic beings, galactic beings or ascended masters. We also have animals that choose to become our spirit guides.

How to connect to your spirit guides is one of the most common things that I get asked. In my individual sessions, I connect to spirit guides and bring through their messages and guidance for individuals. However, I feel that an important part of people living in connection with the Divine is learning to connect with their own guides and getting direct guidance from them. I believe that we all have the ability to do this.

There are various ways in which you can connect to your guides. Some people find it easier than others and some days you will find it easier than other days. I would advise that you be gentle with yourself and remember, just like learning how to ride a bike, it is a process. This takes time. For me, it is a process of remembering how to connect, how to receive this information and how to open ourselves up once again and be able to communicate telepathically. I believe that we all have had different lifetimes where we have communicated telepathically without the need for words. So, try and see this as a journey of self-discovery, a re-learning of a skill that you used to have and don't put pressure on yourself.

I like to separate connecting with spirit guides into two categories:

- How they can connect with us, and
- How we can connect with them.

How they can connect with us

Our spirit guides regularly send us signs to let us know that they are there. They send messages of reassurance and comfort just so that we know that we are not alone. These messages remind us that they are with us and that we are fully supported. Some of the ways that they like to connect with us are:

- *Signs like feathers, animals, birds.*

Feathers are a very common way for our guides to send that message of reassurance to let us know that we are not alone. Your guides will leave you feathers in strategic places so that you see them and know that your guides are reaching out. I tend to find that white feathers are from angelic beings or loved ones in spirit. Other coloured feathers will be from different guides. For example, brown-coloured feathers may be from an indigenous guide such as a Native American.

My guides often send me messages in the form of birds when I am driving in the car. They know that my awareness is taken to birds flying in the sky or hopping at the side of the road, so they have discovered that this is an excellent way to get my attention. The messages may be general ones of comfort and reassurance or sometimes, in my case, they may be more detailed messages that they wish to impart. It is fair to mention that at these times, when my attention is firmly focused on a bird in the sky, it often crosses my mind, who is actually driving the car?

If your guides send you messages in the form of animals or birds, I find it useful to research their spiritual meaning to gain a greater understanding of the message (go to www.kirstielilith.com/book-resources for recommended websites and books).

- *Songs on the radio*

I find this a really useful and easy way for our guides to send us messages. It is a particularly common method if you listen to the radio a lot either in the house or car, or you listen to music on a shuffle playlist. I find that your guides will draw your attention to a particular lyric that will resonate in some way with what is going on for you. This form of communication allows for a deeper level of message than just leaving a sign. Through the lyrics, they are able to get actual worded messages of guidance to you.

My guides have devised an ingenious way of communicating with me through songs. I am not very clairvoyant, so I don't 'see' my guides clearly and unless I am working and actively tuning into my guides, I tend to be closed off to the energies around me. Although this is a good self-care practice as it conserves my energy, it is not always conducive to allowing my guides to connect with me when they have the need. Yet, my guides have cunningly devised a way around me 'switching off' our communication channels! My guides have taken their habit of sending me messages through lyrics in a song to a whole other level! Each one of my main guides has chosen a song that is associated with them. So, whenever I hear the song specific to one guide, I know who wishes to connect with me. I have to say, this works like a dream for me! I don't even have to be listening to music, they can place the song in my head and all of a sudden, it's on a loop until I make time to speak with them. The trick for me now though is actually remembering which song relates to which guide as my memory is not as good as it once was!

- *Recurring numbers*

Guides will often draw our attention to a recurring number sequence on various devices, for example, on digital clocks, on the microwave, oven, radio or in the car. These can be the same numbers, such as 1111 or 222. The numbers might also be in the same sequence, such as 1313. In addition to being a reassuring sign that our guides are reaching out, numeric sequences also have a deeper meaning (go to

www.kirstielilith.com/book-resources for recommended sites).

You may find that your guides use a mixture of the above, or you may be aware of other methods that they use to connect with you. Whatever way they send you signs is right for you and your relationship with your own guides. It will basically be any way that they can get your attention. If your awareness is never drawn to lyrics in a song, then they will unlikely use this as a method of communication – it would be a waste of their energy. Similarly, if you would never see a feather on the ground and could quite obliviously walk through even a sea of feathers without the slightest awareness, then again, this method would be pointless! Your guides will use the most efficient way to get your attention and will use ways in which your focus is drawn.

How we can connect with them

It's all well and good our guides being able to send us signs and messages, but it would be lovely if we could establish a two-way communication. It would be helpful if we could instigate communication and also be able to get more detailed messages. In my experience, direct, clear communication with our guides takes practice. We can easily be discouraged and think that we're 'making it up' or 'just not getting it'! I find that building up to direct communication with our guides helps us to gain confidence and to doubt less. The methods that I recommend are the following:

- *Oracle cards*

Oracle cards are such a simple and effective way to directly connect to our spirit guides. There are a huge variety of oracle decks on the market these days and I would advise you to choose a deck that resonates with you. It may be the artwork, the words on the card or even the colour or feel of the card. The more that you resonate with the deck of cards, the more powerful you will find them and the more you will be inclined to use them.

Most card decks come with a guidebook which offers a more in-depth meaning for each card. To use your card deck for the specific purpose of connecting to your guide's guidance, set the intention while shuffling the deck that this is who you wish to receive the guidance from. Then ask whatever question you would like guidance on from your guides. You can either choose a single card or you may prefer to pull a couple of cards. I would encourage you to use the guidebook to gain further insight into the guidance that your team are offering you. Upon selecting the card(s), you should feel a resonance to the card or the words in the guidebook to the specific question that you asked your guides. When you pick a card, please don't ignore it and place it back in the deck if you don't like it! Often, our guides will tell us something that we maybe don't wish to hear or wasn't the answer we were expecting. It is very tempting to ignore the guidance and pretend that the card came out by accident!

- *Meditation*

The use of meditation is an excellent tool to gain guidance from our guides. This can be done either using a guided meditation (there are

several free guided meditations you can use (go to www.kirstielilith.com/book-resources for recommended meditations) or just to drop into meditation (in whatever way is right for you) If you prefer to meditate in a different way, I suggest the following steps:

1. Make sure you are grounded, either seated with both feet on the floor or standing with the support of a wall.
2. Close your eyes, if you can, or if you prefer to have them open, soften your gaze so you're not focusing on one object.
3. Bring your attention to your breathing and allow any thoughts that you may have to drift through your mind without the need to focus on them.

Once you're in a meditative state, set the intention to connect with your guides. Meditation allows you to go into an altered state of awareness so that your conscious mind is less active and less likely to interfere with the process of connecting with your guides. During this state, your mind is quietened (or better yet, silenced) and you can start building up a relationship with your guides and gain access to their infinite wisdom.

- *Direct communication*

Direct communication is the most effective way of communicating with our guides but also carries the greatest degree of doubt in the information we are receiving. It requires you to move your conscious mind to one side and directly connect with your guide/guides. This communication allows you to ask whatever questions or topics you wish to receive guidance on and to receive your guides' responses. As a result, you need a lot more trust in yourself and your ability to get clear and concise guidance. I believe that we all possess the ability to directly communicate with our guides. It just requires a willingness to learn and to practice, as the old adage goes, Rome wasn't built in a day! I do find that when learning this skill, our guides are more than willing to give us validation of the messages that we receive from them. You will usually find that you receive the same information in a different way just to provide confirmation that your intuition and the message you received were valid, allowing your confidence to grow.

By practising the above ways of connecting with your spirit guides, you will gradually, over time, develop trust in yourself and in the guidance received. Through consistent and intentional practise, you can be encouraged to act on the guidance that you receive more willingly. The more that you act on your guidance and see how things work out in perfect timing, the more your confidence will grow to keep on living this way. It is okay to ask questions and to sometimes doubt the guidance that you are getting. Initially, your guides will provide you with as much proof as possible, but you will eventually be expected to act on faith without the need for proof.

Chapter 5

Kali

Welcome, my dearest sisters and brothers. I welcome you here to this space with me. It is a pleasure and an honour to be able to converse with you, to be given this opportunity to share my views on living in conjunction with the Divine - to allow yourself to fully surrender to living in accordance with your higher self and your soul's purpose. This is the main reason that you incarnated here on Earth; to be able to experience living in a human body while being fully aligned and connected to the Divine, receiving guidance to assist you in flowing smoothly in life. To allow this ease of flow requires trust, but as humans, you so often think that you know best - that your way is best and that you can get things done quicker on your own. In fact, the opposite is true. When you step in at times, thinking that you know better than the Divine, you actually slow the process down. You create roadblocks in your path and the smooth-flowing and guided path that was leading towards whichever direction you were going is now bumpy and full of potholes. You often get in your own way. I completely understand that you have total free will, but it can become very frustrating when you are asking for guidance and to be shown the way and then decide things are not happening fast enough and wade in - the result being that things are just slowed right down. This is where trust comes in - ultimate trust in the Divine, the understanding that there is a higher purpose and reason for everything as well as there being perfect divine timing. Ultimate trust involves stepping back and allowing the Divine to work through you in whatever way and time frame is necessary. It is difficult to totally trust, to let go of control and to allow the Divine to express itself through you in whatever way is necessary. It is not easy letting go of control; that is one of the reasons that many fear working with me as they have to relinquish control as they embark on a journey with me.

Chaotic energy is required at times to be able to create transformation. I encourage people to transform, to completely change their lives and to embrace their full potential. This is not comfortable, and this is not easy. It involves a very high level of trust. Trust in me and trust that everything is going to be okay. When you are in the middle of a huge transformation, it is very hard to cling to the notion that everything is going to be okay as it feels like your whole life is coming crashing around you. But know that you are always held. You are always supported. You are never abandoned, no matter how you feel or what the evidence suggests. Know that we are with you. Know that you are being lovingly supported as you transition through this change. These transitions allow you to shed whatever needs to be shed to bring you closer to alignment with your own divinity. It is only when these layers are cleared from your life that your perspective changes and you have a much clearer view of who you are. It is when this perspective changes that you are able to access your true self, that part of yourself that is masked sometimes, with the careful constructs that you have built in your life. Your true self is completely hidden. It is these spiritual awakenings and transformations that allow you the possibility of connecting to this part of yourself. These channels are required to become clear before you can clearly and consistently connect with your own divinity. It is when you achieve this state that you will be able to trust and surrender to an even deeper level. Allow me to assist you in this process. Allow me to clear aspects of your life that no longer serve you. Allow me to walk beside you during this process. You are safe.

Chapter 6

My Animal Journey

My journey as an animal communicator began in 2015 when I had the opportunity to meet one at my horse's livery yard. An animal communicator is someone who is able to talk to animals – a modern-day 'Dr Dolittle' if you like. From the outset, I knew, on a soul level, that I was meant to do this work, so my training began the very next month. I took to it like a duck to water. Over time, I built up my experience and confidence until I felt that I was at the point where I could offer my services professionally. In my 'paid' work, I mainly work with dogs, cats and horses but over the years, I have had the more unusual requests of rats, chickens and goats! Just like with my human clients, there is no typical work that I do with animals. Sometimes, the animal needs healing from abuse it may have suffered from a past home. Other times, it might be to share a message with the owner. I love my animal work and I consider it such a privilege to be able to communicate with these sentient beings and give them a voice where otherwise they might not have been heard. I also find that my work really helps the animal owners to better understand their animals on a much deeper level.

As with all spiritual work, my animal communication has developed over the years and these days, a lot of the animals show themselves to me as their powerful selves, rather than just as their animal selves. The first time I met the 'unhidden' animal, I was so shocked, I didn't know what to make of it. A friend's dog that was sitting in front of me started morphing into an Egyptian priestess! Nowadays, I have learnt to trust what I am being shown, but back then, I needed a minute or so to collect myself and get over my initial shock before chatting to this 'priestess'.

Today, a lot of my sessions typically result in me chatting with the likes of high priestesses, monks, druids, witches and so on! I love that these beautiful beings show me the lifetimes that they have had, sometimes connected with and alongside their current owners. In addition, they usually show me the lifetime where both animals and humans made the soul contract to be together in this lifetime. Understanding what our animals have chosen to help and guide us through in this lifetime is fascinating. They offer far more than just being our loving companion, a tail wag when we walk through the door after a busy day in the office or cuddles when we're watching TV.

Just when I feel that I have reached a sense of comfort and normality within my work, Spirit steps in to take my work and experiences to a whole new level! One such of these large events happened to me in 2019, when, out of the blue, I had a lioness show up in my energy. One morning, as I was meditating in my lounge, I felt a shiver and sensed another presence. The presence felt different to that of my spirit guides and when I opened my awareness, I discovered it was a lioness. This lioness, however, was not in the spirit world. She was connecting with me from whatever country she was living in. She wanted help transitioning from this life back to spirit. I had never experienced anything like this before in my life and to say I was thrown into a tailspin was an understatement. I tried to ignore her, thinking it was a hallucination, but she wouldn't go away. Had I finally lost my mind? Had I crossed a line between sane and insane? How did I help an animal essentially die when she appeared to be a figment of my imagination? I did not have a clue what I was doing or even if this was real. I tried to help her in whatever way I could and just prayed that I had made a difference. After doing what I felt was my best to support the lioness, the floodgates opened.

From that point on, every single day, I had animals showing up to me energetically wanting some sort of help. I had polar bears, lions, tigers, dolphins, whales and wolves reaching out to me energetically, requesting help for some kind of transition or healing. I don't think that there were many species of wild animals that I didn't have come through and connect with me. Some of these animals were in captivity, while others lived in the wild. All needed my help in some way, shape or form. For me, it was a steep learning curve and, again, I had no feedback as to if I was helping, all I had was a deep desire to make a difference for these beings. Curiously, I didn't know how they were finding me – it was like I had a huge neon sign flashing above my head saying, 'Need animal help? Stop here!'

To be perfectly honest, I spent the majority of that year thinking I'd gone completely crazy! I really thought that I had finally lost the plot and I struggled to talk to anyone about it. I felt voicing it out loud would only make it sound even more cuckoo than it did in my head. So, I just continued fumbling my way through, trying to help as many of these animals as possible. During this time, a pack of wolves became my guides and helped me to prioritise which animals needed urgent help and how to help them. I suppose they were a bit like triage at Accident & Emergency in hospital; developing a sense of who needed more urgent attention than others! Healing and helping the spirits of animals became my day-to-day life for quite a while. The number of different animals with different needs was quite mind-blowing. From trauma from being locked in a cage to mourning the loss of their child, I helped them in whatever capacity I could. The most upsetting for me were the animals that were located in testing facilities; it took all my strength to remain emotionally neutral so that I could effectively help.

I have found that if you are prepared to walk an unknown spiritual path in blind faith, the Spirit will usually step forward with some sort of verification. The first few steps are the most daunting, because you must be willing to walk alone, without the need for validation. This comes later. My validation came when I was receiving a spiritual reading with an American lady and the woman suddenly stopped mid-flow and asked quizzically, 'This is going to sound very odd, but do you have a pack of wolves living with you?' That sentence changed my life because it validated what I knew all along. I began to accept that maybe I was not crazy, and my future did not involve a mental institution after all. The relief was massive. The fact that she had picked up on my energetic pack of wolves made me feel that maybe this WAS happening and that maybe I was not making it up after all. This confirmation from her gave me the confidence to continue walking my path with a renewed sense of purpose.

It was during this year that I had the privilege of becoming 'mummy' to two beautiful kittens (yes, actual real kittens!). Their names are Sabrina and Phoenix, and they definitely chose to be with me and help and guide me. From our first few meetings, they shared that they are from the same planet as me, Arcturus, and we have had many lifetimes together. All three of us are Star Beings (which is a term used for a 'being' originating from a different planet or star system) and chose to reunite again at this point in time on Earth. Sabrina is amazingly connected to all forms of beings and her 'task' involves a lot of downloading of codes and frequencies (both into me and the crystalline grid of Earth). Phoenix is a Master Healer, and as well as helping me, he often assists in providing healing to clients. I am blown away every day by what my two cats are willing to do for me as they assist me on my journey. From the moment they arrived, they helped take my healing and awareness to a new level. They showed me how to use galactic technology to help heal animals, both in the physical realm and energetically.

At this time, many captive animals came to me energetically that were struggling with the stress of captivity. I was shown how to teach these animals to take their consciousness to their natural environment. Our mind, our consciousness is always free and unlimited. I taught these animals to remember this important point, and that this mindset allows them the freedom of being back in the wild. We always have a choice of how we react to our external circumstances and animals are no different. This revelation was literally life-changing for some of these animals, knowing that they were not bound by the physical limits of their existence. They had the potential to transport their awareness back to the ocean, the jungle or wherever they chose.

On the subject of captive animals, I feel the need to share my philosophy. I believe that the souls of these animals have chosen to experience captivity in their lifetime. I believe that no animal is captive that didn't choose to be there at some level (whether conscious or subconscious). This does not mean that it is right that they are in captivity, and that we can treat them cruelly. Personally, I would love animals to be able to live wild and free in their natural habitat. However, I do feel that some aspects of captivity have its time and place. One such example is helping endangered species thrive in an ever-increasing hostile environment. I have been guided over the last few years to visit wildlife parks to help various animals and to allow them to cope better with their captive environment. When talking to some of these animals, they have shared their reasons for being captive with me. Some wish to experience captivity for their own soul's growth. Some remain caged to raise humanity's consciousness by being able to have access to humans which, in the wild, would not normally be possible. Many people would not have the opportunity to see a tiger, for example, unless in a wildlife park or zoo. Animals have the ability to change us at a cellular level and these animals often choose to interact with us, allowing us to grow and elevate as a species. They raise our awareness and as a result, there have been many changes in recent years around the care of animals in captivity. As with the majority of things, there is usually a mixture of reasons, but I feel that this is one of them. It never ceases to amaze me what animals are prepared to do for us and our greater good, and it humbles me every day to see their selflessness and how far they are prepared to go to see our planet and us, as a species, ascend.

Spirit always brings the right people to you at the right time. During that year, I was guided to a book called 'The Whale Whisperer', written by a woman named Madeleine Walker. (go to www.kirstielilith.com/book-resources for further information). As far as my animal journey was concerned, that book changed my life. Reading Madeleine's story and her beautiful encounters with animals made me able to understand and accept my path more. Her way of communicating with animals really resonated with my experiences and she allowed me to feel a little less isolated. Her journey with animals also follows a path that would be considered 'outside the norm' and to date, she is the only person that I have met who works in a similar way to me. I had the opportunity of having a couple of online sessions with her during that year which I massively benefited from. When I had the opportunity to attend an animal communication workshop that she was running the following year, I jumped at the chance!

So, in mid-2020, I set off towards the Glastonbury area of the UK to meet the infamous Madeleine Walker. I was so excited, I felt like I was meeting a celebrity. I had read all of her books by then and really resonated with her message. The weekend was inspirational. It did not bother me that I was already a practitioner and on the course with beginners. In my experience, it does not matter at what level you are on your communication journey, the animals are always our greatest teachers, and this weekend was no exception. The workshop was held at a beautiful location just outside Glastonbury that was home to a herd of healing horses. These horses and their owner worked with groups of people, in particular troubled and disadvantaged children. It was an honour to meet this herd and work with them for the weekend.

Chapter 7

Journey with the Whales Begins!

My life and journey are now built completely on trust. Over time, my intuition grew to a level where I could clearly communicate with my guides. I trust my guides implicitly and will follow their guidance without hesitation. I am not suggesting that this is always smart, as my sharing of my journey with the whales in this book will testify to. Following my guides fully is how I live in connection with the Divine. In 2021, I was asked to deepen my 'TRUST' with my guides. This next phase of my journey was based on complete faith in the guidance that I was receiving and, despite the predicaments that I found myself in at times, I continued following this guidance. I made the decision that I was going to trust the guidance that I was getting and see this journey through, no matter what they asked of me.

In July 2021, I had my first visit from a humpback whale. One morning, sipping my tea on the sofa and preparing for what I thought would be a typical day, I felt the presence of a rather large humpback whale! I don't hear words, but the resounding feeling left me with the words 'connect with me'. Like most interactions with spirits, I agreed, internally saying 'Of course'. Closing my eyes, I tuned into the whale's energy. Feeling the whale's energy enter and mix with my own energy felt so powerful and yet, almost familiar. The whale took me into his vision, where I was transported high above the earth, and the whole world appeared as a blue globe surrounded by dark space. He then showed us connecting with different groups of whales across the whole of the planet and all of us being connected together with beams of light that stretched around the earth like a web. It was absolutely stunning to see how all of these species, as well as us humans, are interconnected in perfect unity. Each group of whales that was present in this vision started singing to me in their beautiful, unique tones. Hearing the deep resonance and higher tones from each group felt as if every cell of my body was vibrating in resonance with their singing. It was an absolutely phenomenal experience. After the vision ended, I cried with utter joy from the immense experience of hearing the whale frequencies and having energetically connected to them.

A few days later, the same whale appeared to me and asked me to connect with him again. Of course, I jumped at the opportunity. During this connection, he announced that he wanted me to physically come and find him and that I needed to go and swim with him in the water. Slightly unsure of this guidance, I asked 'So, you want me to find one whale in an entire planet of oceans?' His response was a simple 'Yes,' and then he left! I sat in my room for a while feeling stunned, pondering on what had just happened. Coming out of my meditation with this new guidance, I was shocked and nervous. Since an early age, I've been afraid of the sea, especially deep water where I can't see the bottom, so the thought of deliberately putting myself in the ocean, knowing that an enormous whale was there with me, petrified me. There was also the added complication that I live in the UK and, apart from a few sightings of orcas and minke whales, we don't get many whales, so the likelihood of one of these being my whale was pretty slim. How on earth was I going to find this whale, let alone overcome my fear of the ocean?!

Did I think I was crazy for even contemplating trusting this guidance at times? Most definitely. Did I sometimes think I was idiotic for actually following the guidance and following the voice of a whale? Without a doubt! But – I kept going, I kept trusting and I kept believing in the Divine.

Always up for a challenge, and the whale having piqued my curiosity, I reached out to my guides who I knew could help me. Trying to search for one whale when I had no idea where he resided, along with the awareness that whales don't have permanent addresses and can swim hundreds of miles, made it feel like the weirdest game of hide-and-seek I'd ever played! My guides guided me to reach out to someone in America who I've previously worked with. Calling her, I explained the situation and asked if she had any idea of where I should start looking for my whale.

Miracle number one: a few days after we had spoken, she messaged me to advise that I should contact a woman in Hawaii and gave me her contact details.

Miracle number two: scrolling through this Hawaiian woman's website, I felt the blood drain from my face and tingles down my spine, as I started reading about a Cosmic Golden Ray whale called Nagwal. I instantly knew that this was my whale. This whale, Nagwal, is seen as the communicator for all whales and was born in 2015. According to her website, she was running a retreat starting in September 2021, in Moorea, an island off Tahiti. During this retreat, people would have the opportunity to swim with the humpback whales. I knew this was where Nagwal wanted me to go. With less than two months to go until the retreat started, and the retreat already showing as 'fully booked, I knew that if I was meant to be on this retreat, the power was in the universe and a place would open up for me.

Miracle number three: I chose to send the woman an email expressing my interest in being on her retreat and within a few short days, she replied to say that she'd made the decision to postpone her upcoming retreat for 12 months, and due to this decision, one of her clients had dropped out. This meant that, as long as I was available the following year, September 2022, I could attend!

On some levels, I couldn't believe what had just happened. Within weeks of the first connection with Nagwal, I had actually located him, knew his name AND I was booked onto a retreat to swim with him! I was so ecstatic. It was difficult to comprehend and get my head around the fact I would actually be swimming with these magnificent creatures, up close and personal, in the Pacific Ocean. Plus, I would be able to visit the beautiful islands of Tahiti and Moorea. I felt like the luckiest person in the world! I started doing the conga down my hallway singing 'I'm going to Tahiti' at the top of my voice in celebration! The power of surrendering to the Divine had led me to the simplest hide-and-seek ever... but my journey wasn't quite over...

Two 'minor' issues then occurred to me at this point:

One, I don't like boats as I get very seasick.

Two, I don't like swimming in the ocean due to fear of being eaten by sharks. (The film, Jaws, has a lot to answer for, I can tell you!)

As these two fears entered my mind, the dancing and singing came to an abrupt halt. I felt my airways restrict as panic started to set in.

As soon as my breath got shorter, my guides immediately came through and told me to just relax, keep breathing and let go of any overwhelm; everything would be okay. So, I did.

The following month, Jesus, my main guide, came through during meditation as normal, but this morning, he shared with me that the work that I would be doing in Tahiti with Nagwal was to complete a soul contract made between us many thousands of years ago regarding Divine Union. As explained previously, Divine Union is the perfect balance between the Divine Feminine and the Divine Masculine. Jesus explained that I was going to represent the Divine Feminine vessel and Nagwal was going to represent the Divine Masculine. When the two of us came together, in person, and connected we were going to birth the Divine Masculine energy back on this planet. This was the soul contract that Nagwal and I had agreed to all those millennia ago. All I knew previously about the Divine Masculine is that this energy needs to be birthed through the Divine Feminine energy, so it slightly made sense to me on a theoretical basis. On a practical level, my mind was struggling to comprehend the enormity of the mission... birth the Divine Masculine? Me? Of course, no problem! No pressure there then! My little self started berating my higher self as to what on Earth she had signed us up for! I had a huge mission in front of me which included seasickness and sharks... What could possibly go wrong? But with my usual pragmatic nature, I decided they were worries for another day. The retreat was over twelve months away, so there was no point in stressing myself out just yet. I also convinced myself that there was no way that the Divine would just entrust this mission to me. They wouldn't be stupid enough to put all their eggs in one basket, so to speak. They would get several people to do similar missions all around the world just in case one person failed, right?

Whenever the significance of this trip felt too overwhelming, I would just repeat this to myself:

'I am one of many people across the planet being divinely guided to complete this task.'

After my message/communication with Jesus, Nagwal came through to share that our journey together was just beginning. He showed our interlocking paths stretching out from this point into the future, just like stepping stones. At key points along this journey, we would unite to complete some kind of task. These tasks would be revealed to me when the time was right. The culmination of our journey would be the ultimate mission in Tahiti in September of the following year. The way forward seemed to be getting slightly clearer even though I had no idea what these 'tasks' were or how they fitted into the bigger plan. Plus, how on earth did one 'birth the Divine masculine'?

At this point, I wish to share a bit about Nagwal and what a privilege it is to share this journey with him. It is not something that I take lightly, and I feel so humbled and grateful to be doing this 'mission' with him. To me, his energy is very powerful and intense. It is like being hit by a brick wall of raw power. It's hard to miss when he enters my energy field! I work a lot with the Divine Masculine and the range in which this energy can present itself is quite large. Jesus, for example, has a very gentle divine energy and whilst still powerful, he has a distinct softness to it. Nagwal has no softness to his energy. He is full of strength and power and in his full divinity. I found it fascinating to experience this masculine power and I'm very grateful that I got to explore these subtle nuances of the Divine Masculine energies.

Nagwal was born in 2015, in the Pacific Ocean, near Tonga. A friend and fellow animal communicator, Madeleine Walker (mentioned in a previous chapter), got to witness his conception first-hand. Well, to rephrase, she was in the ocean as his parents dived deep down beneath her to conceive Nagwal. As she got back onto the boat, the two whales breached again and again in joyous celebration and union. Madeleine had previously received clear guidance from his mother, Nazru, that Nagwal would be conceived on the Full Pink Moon and would be the communicator of all whales. She never anticipated though that she would have the privilege of being there in person. Nagwal had first presented himself to Madeleine back in 2008, in energetic form, as a very powerful prehistoric being. Madeleine shares her fascinating encounters with Nagwal (as well as her adventures with numerous animals) in one of her many books, The Whale Whisperer.

Nagwal was unique from an early age and displayed unprecedented behaviour for a humpback whale. As a month-old calf, he notoriously led the charging heat run with many males vying to mate with his mother. This has never been witnessed before as such a young calf would always be by the side of his mother. This type of behaviour demonstrated that he was indeed a Master Avatar Whale. It was such an honour to be working with this amazing being.

One of the significant stepping stones on my journey with Nagwal was that in August 2021, I was divinely guided to move to a property situated very close to the River Trent in the UK. I had no idea that this river's destiny and mine were so intertwined and would play a significant role in my unfolding path with Nagwal. I discovered that the river was tidal, which made sense as to why she was connected with my work with the whales. I was guided to conduct a sacred opening ceremony with the Trent and consciously connect with her. How I connect with nature, such as rivers, is akin to how I connect with my guides. I allowed my energy to extend outwards with the intention of connecting with her. She welcomed me with such gratitude and love, it was very humbling. After this, I began working with her on a daily basis.

Another guided trip was to Glastonbury, UK, in January 2022. Glastonbury is steeped in the mystical energy of Avalon. Nagwal requested that I take a sample of water from the Trent and meet up there with a friend from France, who had also been guided to bring water from her local river. We were guided to place these water samples in the wells at Glastonbury. This was the first time that I had encountered the issue of collecting water from the Trent. This act sounds very easy in principle but is not so easy in practice! She is a very wide river, with high banks. I quickly recognised, not being the most coordinated being on the planet, that this was going to be quite a challenge for me. Visions of me toppling headfirst into the river became an imminent reality. I decided reinforcements were needed, so called a local friend who very kindly agreed to assist me. She had the agility of a mountain goat and was much more suited to the task at hand!

Once in Glastonbury, I followed the guiding messages to collect a third water sample from the White Spring (masculine energy) before going to the Red Spring, the Chalice Well, which is the feminine energy. At the Chalice Well, we conducted a ceremony. We opened up the sacred space and both of us called in our guides to assist. With reverence, we both took turns depositing the water samples that we had collected. The stillness in the space surrounding us while we conducted this ceremony felt both electric and magical. We then received the guidance that to complete the ceremony, it was important that we collected water both from the Chalice Well and the White Spring to take back to our respective rivers.

The transferal of water samples from one source to another is very important. It was shared with me by my guides that the cross-pollination of energy and information between water sources could take place through the simple action of water-sharing. Throughout the year, I was asked to 'cross-pollinate' a lot of rivers, oceans and other water sources. I was guided to take 'codes' from the Trent and 'deposit' them in a variety of rivers across the UK. I would then connect with these rivers and take 'codes' back to the Trent. So, there was a lot of transfer of information and energy throughout the year among key waterways across Britain. My work with the water seemed all-consuming, but I knew that it was a necessary part of my journey, working with the whales. This work was about me trusting my guidance and carrying out what I was asked to do, even though some of it made little sense to me.

So, that was how my journey with Nagwal began. The retreat was booked. My flights to Tahiti were booked. The accommodation was sorted. I will never forget that moment on the plane though when I allowed myself to ponder on what it was going to be like swimming in the ocean, off the coast of Moorea. My mind started to envision getting into the deep ocean with the whales – whoa... Wait ...What? Me... in the ocean? My heart dropped into my stomach, and I broke out in a cold sweat as I realised a stark truth. I'd never been swimming in the ocean before. Oh god, maybe I should have thought about this before now.

Part Three

CONTROL & BOUNDARIES

Chapter 8

Control

> *When you can't control what's happening, challenge yourself to control the way you respond to what's happening.*
>
> *That's where your power is!*
>
> — *Unknown*

As humans, we don't like the concept of letting go of control. The irony is that in reality, we have very little control over anything. But we still like to cling to the fantasy that we do have control over our life, over situations and other people. We think if we hold on really tight to people or situations and don't let go, it gives us a feeling of some sort of control. We think if we try hard enough or put enough intent or thought into things then we can somehow control the outcome.

The only control we have is within ourselves and how we choose to respond to situations. We can't choose what happens to us, but we can choose how to react to it. Let me repeat that again. You can't choose what happens to you, but you can choose how to react to it.

In each and every situation that happens to you in life, you have absolute control over how you choose to respond to it. WOW. Doesn't that sound freeing - you do have control and you do have a choice, you just need to consciously decide how to choose to act. This is completely different from trying to control every aspect of your life. This is about recognising that you don't have control over anything external to you, but you always can choose how you respond. This is what you have control of. This is where your power lies. For example, the weather – how often do people think they can control the weather, or we let the weather control our reaction? If it's raining, you have absolutely no control over this, but you can choose to feel gratitude for the plants being watered or you can choose to feel relaxed by the sound the raindrops make on the window. It's all about choice.

The quicker we learn this simple fact, the easier and happier our lives become. When we let go of that need to control situations and realise that 'control' is just an illusion, we can start to flow more with life. We can start to allow more ease and grace into our lives. This allows the Divine to work through us much more easily as we stop resisting and 'controlling' the direction of our lives and start to move out of the way so they can guide us more.

When we first try and let go of some of the control over our lives, it can feel quite disorientating. It is a bit like being a river. There are white water rapids, where we are being buffeted around at the mercy of the water. We are so used to trying to hold onto passing trees and boulders in the river (aka trying to control our lives) that when we first let go it feels very disorientating and very uncomfortable. Yet, in a river, this is what we need to do; the more we surrender to the river and flow with the water, the more we are able to see the direction of our travel, and, with very small changes and positions of our body, we can glide past the boulders and towards smoother water. The more that we practise 'letting go of control', accepting life and situations as they are and consciously choosing how to react to situations rather than trying to control the situation, life becomes a lot less chaotic.

This is not about 'giving up' or thinking that you're accepting 'failure'. It is about recognising that the control you thought you had was only an illusion. Using the analogy of the river again, it feels like moving into a stretch of calm water, a steady flow of water. One where we go with the current, rather than against it and allow the current to gently manoeuvre us around boulders or 'blocks' in our life that present themselves. Life becomes more about flow and being efficient with your energy. It is about seeing your life through a different lens. Observe the situations in your life and start to recognise where you are placing your energy and where you are trying to control external influences. Take time to reflect on where you could respond differently and where you could let the reins go and let some of that need to control go. Initially, it will feel uncomfortable, but the more that you practise it, the more familiar it will feel.

Part of letting go of control is about understanding what is down to you and what belongs to others. We expend a lot of energy in trying to control the people in our lives; trying to control situations so as to minimise the impact that other people will have on us, trying to control situations so that we don't upset other people, or they don't react in a certain way that will upset you. Remember, you are not responsible for how other people behave. How other people behave or are triggered by you is not your responsibility. You have no say over that and no control over that. You can only control how you behave and how you respond to situations. Understanding this key point is vital to being able to let go and flow with the Divine. We take on so much responsibility, without even realising it, in trying to manage other people's reactions and expectations. It's time to quit. Allow them to manage their own reactions. That is where their power is and where their control is. It is time for you to focus on you.

Chapter 9

Nagwal

Dearest fellow beings, we meet again. It is a pleasure to be able to come forward and connect with you and share my views on the topic of Divine Living. I am a cosmic being that has travelled the universe for millennia. I have lived in many different incarnations with a variety of vibrations. The incarnations where I have been able to choose to live in connection with the Divine have been the most satisfying. This type of living brings a certain sense of peace and fulfilment. It is the most natural state that we can achieve while in a physical body that brings us closest to our true nature. It may feel difficult or alien for you to be living in this way or attempting these teachings, but I can assure you that this type of living or being is the only way that aligns with your true state. It is ultimately who you are. When you start to experience glimpses of this way of being it feels like you are coming home. In a way, you are actually coming home - home to yourself. It provides you with a deep sense of fulfilment.

So, I would encourage you all to keep trying to align with this way of living, to practise each day until it becomes more familiar and finally becomes your default setting. You all have the ability to achieve this state of living in connection with your divinity, I can assure you of this, so do not give up. I would also urge you to adopt a sense of lightness and freedom in your journey of self-discovery. It is easy to get lost on the path and allow it to consume you and become heavy, to get fixated on the destination, become blinkered and lose sight of what is important. It is not about getting it right and feeling like a failure if you don't live up to this imaginary yardstick. It is more like visualising this journey as an adventure and giving yourself permission to explore a new direction and new way of being with a sense of fun and excitement. It is waking up every day with a child-like wonder of endless possibilities, allowing yourself to relax and flow with life rather than trying to push for an imaginary outcome. It is seeing each day as another opportunity to practise a new way of being, whilst also acknowledging that it isn't really a 'new' way of being, it is just a 'remembering' of a way that you have achieved many times as a soul.

Viewing your journey from this perspective allows you the opportunity to not get caught in the trap of 'right' and 'wrong' or 'winning' and 'failing'. It relieves you of the pressure of constantly feeling like you are failing and are just not 'getting it'. When you are able to change your perspective and not view your life in these terms, but as an exciting adventure of 'what ifs', your whole life will shift. The energy of 'what if' opens you up to new possibilities and allows you the freedom to fully explore this way of being more from a heart space than a head space. When you can shift your perspective in this way, you truly start to align with your true self. Life switches from being a chore to being fun. Being aligned to the divine energies is like flowing with a river rather than trying to swim upstream all the time. Your life will take on new meaning and purpose. You will feel like you know yourself better, your true self. There will be a contentment deep within where there used to be a feeling of discontentment and not belonging. You truly will feel like you have arrived home. I will be walking this path with you as you make your way home once again, shining a light, illuminating your next step and highlighting the path of least resistance. When you reach this awakened state of being and have fully arrived home, I will be there to greet you, dear ones.

Chapter 10

Letting Go of Control

Before I even left for Tahiti, I had to work on letting go of control and establishing boundaries. I have experienced many situations where I have been asked to let go of control and to make the conscious choice of how I react. The lesson of letting go of control is one that keeps cropping up for me, time and time again. In different situations and different scenarios, it is highlighted to me to keep letting go of that illusion of control. One day, I was put in a situation which allowed me the opportunity to walk my talk and to choose how I responded rather than trying to control the external influences.

One of the challenges that I continued to face during my time working with the river Trent was how to get water samples from her safely. I was asked to collect water from her for various reasons and each time, I encountered a different set of challenges. To reduce the number of challenges I would encounter, I nearly always visited the rivers that Nagwal wanted me to collect samples from prior to the actual event. Yet, this preemptive preparation didn't always work and on one Tuesday afternoon, I arrived at what I knew to be an empty field. However, instead of a leisurely stroll across a clover paddock, I was greeted with a herd of cows lying down under a tree in the corner of the field. I appreciate that cows aren't seen as predators or naturally aggressive, but they can cause quite serious damage to people if they are spooked or protecting their young, people like a woman meandering towards the local river,

Standing by the gate, observing the herd and mulling over the safety aspects of entering the field, I noted that there were a couple of calves, yet all the cows were lying down and a reasonable distance away from the gate and river. Also, I couldn't see any sign of a bull. My trust that Nagwal wouldn't put me in danger's way was needed at this time, so I started devising a plan on how to get to the river safely. I decided that if I walked along the edge of the field, keeping as much distance as possible between myself and the cows, I could make it to the cove area of the river without disrupting the cows or piquing their interest enough for them to come over to me. My plan worked beautifully! I made it to the cove without any drama and happily collected the water sample I needed. As you can probably start to guess, the next phase of my plan didn't go so well. The farmer arrived at the field in his tractor and headed straight towards the cows. His loud tractor moving quickly towards the herd resulted in them all getting up from their afternoon sleep and starting to move around the field. I tried to make my way back out of the field the same way that I came but unfortunately, the cows spotted me and became curious. Just a point to note here - cows can move really fast when they want to! I quickly realised that there was no way I could reach the gate before the cows got to me. On reflection, I don't think even an Olympic sprinter could have made it! Cows with calves are quite unpredictable and they are also very curious and think nothing of running on mass. The faster I walked, the faster the cows moved, and panic started to set in about my predicament. I looked wildly around me at my limited options of escape, as the cows came increasingly closer.

One option was to go into the river, but I realised that if I could easily get into the water, so could the cows! I decided now was not the time to test the theory of whether cows like water. The second option meant I would need to jump in the ditch, which separated the two large fields. As I looked into the ditch, all I could see was a lot of nettles and I also couldn't check if there was water at the bottom. This option was not at all enticing, but as I looked at the herd of cows running towards me getting ever closer, I was left with no choice, and into the ditch, I went!

It was at this point I realised that I had to surrender control. There was no way of controlling this situation. As I stood in this ditch, which luckily had no water in it, looking upwards at the many cow faces peering down at me, I pondered my stupidity. Firstly, I realised my mobile phone was safely on the front seat of my car and secondly, no one knew where I was. I also had no idea if the cows could follow me into the ditch as some of them were beginning to look like they might try. I concluded that I had no control whatsoever over the predicament that I found myself in, but I did recognise that I had a choice of how to respond to it.

I did have complete control over whether I responded to this situation from a place of hysteria or calmness. I chose the latter. I started to calm myself down and get my breathing back to a normal rhythm. It then occurred to me that I did have an advantage over a lot of people in this scenario – I could talk to animals! I needed to regulate my breathing before I could even attempt to tune in. An acute adrenalin rush is not an optimal state for animal communication! When I did finally tune in, it was laughable really. The ones peering down on me were all saying, 'What on earth are you doing down there?' As the next lot pushed their way to the viewing point, all I could hear was 'You're right, it is Kirstie – what are you doing down there?' They could not comprehend that I was down here escaping from them! It was like I had become the best entertainment ever and they were not in any rush to move on so, I spent the rest of my time in the ditch tuned into them asking each of the cows in turn to 'moooo...ve' on over to the little walkway into the next field. I roped all my spirit guides into speaking with the cows as well – well, why not because we all had nothing better to do with our time! It took quite a bit of time to move these cows and, one by one, they moved over into the next field with just the power of tuning in and asking them! I was really impressed that this was working at all because the desire in them to just watch me all day was very strong. On reflection, I don't think cows get a lot of variety entertainment-wise, so my ditch-escapade was proving very popular. The last cow nearly sent me over the edge as it took over twenty minutes to move her. She was very tenacious, to say the least, and she was not going to be rushed.

Finally, when I got her into the next field, I carefully climbed back out of the ditch, peering furtively in all directions before fully committing to being out in the open again. Although the cows were still within reaching distance, I gauged that they were sufficiently bored by me and distracted by eating, so I made a run for it! I never knew I could move that quickly. The adrenaline pumping through my body took ages to subside, even after I was safely in my car. An added bonus was that I had not managed to drop my bottle of water from the Trent, otherwise, I would have had to return to the field of cows to collect another sample! I did decide though, that I did not want to repeat that experience again in a hurry. Surely, there had to be an easier way to do this spiritual work. I drove home, cursing a certain whale!

CHAPTER 11

BOUNDARIES

> *Daring to set boundaries is about*
>
> *having the courage to love ourselves,*
>
> *even when we risk disappointing others.*
>
> — *BRENE BROWN*

One of the key aspects of being able to live in conjunction with your true self is boundaries. A lot of people mistakenly think that when you connect to your true essence and start to live from a place of love, you accept and allow others to do or say whatever they wish to you. The very opposite is true. A big part of living from your heart space is learning to put boundaries in place. True love has very distinct boundaries. It is about being able to radiate out pure, unconditional love to the whole world but also to be able to radiate that love inwards on yourself. The more that you practise self-love, the more you are required to set boundaries.

Self-love is about honouring yourself and deciding how you should be treated. It is about knowing what is acceptable and what is not acceptable. Loving someone unconditionally does not mean that you allow them to treat you badly or disrespectfully. To me, loving yourself and others unconditionally means knowing when to walk away. It is about discernment as well as respect for yourself. Others have a right to see you in whatever light or way is right for them - this is their truth. This does not mean that you have to metaphorically stand there and take this 'opinion' or treatment. It is okay to love someone and move away from them. It is okay to move out of someone's life and decide not to want to have any contact with them. This is discernment, when you decide what is and what is not acceptable behaviour by the people in your life. It is about putting those strong boundaries in place as you move into loving yourself enough to do this.

You, and only you, get to decide what is acceptable treatment. We so often give our power to others and allow them to decide how to treat us, how to speak to us and act towards us. It is time to take your power back. To stop being a doormat. To stop people from thinking it is okay to say and do whatever they want to you. Only you can decide what is acceptable. Only you can create those boundaries.

Sometimes, loving someone is knowing when to say no and when to walk away. It is about knowing when enough is enough. It is not about trying to change other people's mindsets or actions so that they fit or resonate with your own. Everyone is entitled to their own viewpoint and to live from a place that resonates with them, even if this is different to yours. It is okay to love someone and let them go. It may be difficult and feel like a hard decision to make, but when you prioritise loving yourself, placing boundaries in your life becomes very simple. It becomes easier the more that you practise it. People have a right to their own opinions, what they do not have is the right to impose them upon you and force you to take on their opinions as your own. You, and only you, decide what is acceptable and what is not. Walking away is a sign of strength, not weakness. It is a positive aspect when you can live life from a place of discernment.

So often in our relationships, we allow the other to manipulate us, to bully us, to think that it is okay and acceptable that they can say exactly what they wish. This is when the dynamics in relationships become out of balance. True relationships should not be about power, but so often, relationships do end up being about having power over someone. This imbalance is corrected and brought back into balance with the use of personal boundaries. Boundaries are not about building a wall around you that prevents others from getting close. It is about loving and respecting yourself enough so that you will only accept the very best treatment and behaviour. Another way to phrase boundaries is having standards. It is about setting a code of standards for yourself and holding the people in your life lovingly accountable to these standards. It is only when you decide that you deserve the very best treatment that people will start treating you this way. It starts with you; it comes from you. It is only you that can create this set of standards for yourself.

It is not always easy to keep these boundaries in place. With certain people, it will be easier to maintain your boundaries than with others. With particular people in our lives, we can be much more emotionally manipulated and pulled off balance. For example, trying to establish boundaries with our partner or children can prove quite challenging at times. Learn to start placing boundaries in the easier areas of your life first, maybe at work or the gym. As you become more proficient in honouring your boundaries, move to the more difficult areas, such as family members, and start to tackle those areas. Usually, it is the people closest to you that we struggle with the most. This does not mean that it is impossible to have strong boundaries, it just requires a little more discipline and awareness. Just keep practising and taking one step at a time. First comes the awareness of the dynamics of the relationship, then the desire to shift those dynamics and then the strength to implement them. It's a step-by-step process. Even if you make a mistake, learn from it and try again another time.

Chapter 12

Setting Boundaries

Nagwal helped me tremendously in understanding my boundaries, in particular, my dynamics with men and how my energy can be impacted in their presence. He showed me how I had a pattern of 'leaning into' the masculine energy. Nagwal would come in close to my energy and allow me to experience how my energy changed. I would literally 'lean into' his energy. I could feel my energy being pulled towards his like a magnet as I wanted to 'melt' into his masculine energy. Every time I did this, he would yell 'NO! Maintain your boundaries!' He would practise this with me time and time again until I was able to keep my energy centred and not be pulled out of alignment by his energy. Once I was able to maintain my boundaries with him to his satisfaction, he then brought other Divine Masculine beings into my energy so that I could practise the same exercise with them. I could have said no but I surrendered to Nagwal because I knew he had my highest good at heart. It was an amazing opportunity to be in the presence of these Divine Masculine beings whose energies were all unique. Obviously, I didn't get it right every time, but I kept repeating the exercise until I was able to maintain my own energy despite the closeness of these beautiful masculine energies.

How do you start setting boundaries in your life? My advice would be to take the following steps:

1. Start by exploring areas where you feel you are being disrespected and then make the decision that you are going to put boundaries in place. Write down the areas in your life where you feel that people are taking advantage of you or walking all over you. When you are spiritual, you are usually sensitive and sometimes people take this as a sign of weakness. Start by examining the relationships in your life – work, family and friends.
2. Choose one area of your life that you want to work on first. Don't try and tackle your whole life at once as you will easily lose confidence in yourself and your ability to establish robust boundaries. Know that your boundaries will be tested. The people in your life will be like children – they will test you just to establish how resolved you are. Nobody likes it when the goalposts are shifted, or the rules of the game are changed. This is just human nature so be aware of this and know that your decisions will be tested.
3. Become aware of how people in that area are stepping over your boundaries. There are various ways in which people can disrespect you. There are obvious ways such as being rude to you, talking over you, ignoring you and just using you like a doormat, but there are also so many subtle ways that you can be disrespected, ways in which it would be so easy to let slide, to convince yourself that you are imagining it, and they probably didn't mean it that

way. Rule of thumb – if it doesn't make you feel good, it most likely isn't good! Subtle ways could be someone always turning up late or if you've made an agreement about something, changing the rules last minute (for example, if you've arranged a time to have a phone call and the other person rings an hour early). These are all little and subtle things that indicate people are being disrespectful. Another example might be people saying 'funny' things about you to you or other people in your company, comments that just aren't funny and then if you react, being told that you are 'too sensitive'. These are just examples of situations where boundaries need to be put in place. Just know that you get to choose how people treat you, how they talk to you and how they act around you. It is about being able to say no and mean it.

4. Create a plan. After you have established which area or person you are going to tackle first, you then need to have a strategy. I find when putting boundaries in place, it is really advisable to have a pre-prepared plan. It means that you are less likely to be caught off guard and it gives you more confidence when you are taking your first tentative steps. Setting boundaries is not easy – it takes commitment and practice. So have a plan at the ready. Is your strategy to simply say 'no' to the person? *No* is such a little word but can be hard to say and for people to accept it. Placing boundaries is a lot about being able to say 'no' and stick to it. If you want to tackle someone who likes to disrespect you in subtle ways in conversations, maybe have a pre-prepared comment to pull out the bag when this happens so you are not caught off guard.
5. Stand your ground. I have had to put boundaries in place in nearly every area of my life. It is only as you get more

proficient at seeing how others like to test and flex your boundaries that you know how to step up. I find that it is not always obvious and sometimes you need a few reminders before you get the message that your boundaries are being overstepped. It's not that people are necessarily bad or trying to take advantage of you, it's just people don't tend to realise they've overstepped until you make it clear especially if this is a long-standing pattern for them – either with you or just in general. When starting to put boundaries in place, it is about being consistent.

6. Practice honouring your boundaries. I exhibit at a lot of well-being shows and meet a lot of different people. As well as the obvious business connections, I have found they are an excellent opportunity to practise things like boundaries and for me to identify where I am still lacking in this. For example, I give animal readings to people at the shows, and I will tune into either current or past pets as part of the reading. I became aware that, over a period of a few shows, I was attracting people who wanted the readings for free. And I was giving it to them. Sounds insane, right? It took a couple of times before I noticed the pattern and then took action. It was the pulling on my heartstrings that lowered my normally in place boundaries. The dog that had just died. The sick cat. The pet that was being impacted by relationship issues. People 'just wanted to know this', they 'just wanted me to check that they were okay'. I was allowing this, and I was expending my energy and tuning into these animals because of the circumstances and me thinking I can't ask for money because their dog has just died etc. There is nothing wrong with giving away things for free, but it is

about making a conscious choice to do that, not just letting it happen because you feel you can't say no or feel emotionally manipulated. These scenarios (and there have been many more!) have given me the opportunity to decide where my boundaries lie and what I was prepared to and not prepared to accept in these situations.

7. Enjoy learning and growing. It is not about being perfect and getting it right. There is no right or wrong. It is about deciding what is acceptable to you and having some fun while you reclaim your boundaries and learn to say 'no' more.

Part Four

HEALING

Chapter 13

Healing

> *Sometimes, the smallest step in the right direction ends up being the biggest step of your life.*
>
> *Tip toe if you must but take the step.*
>
> — *Affirmations & Quotes*

When we open ourselves up to our spiritual path and purpose, we begin to recognise that there is so much more to life and the universe than what we realise. I consider that a big part of our spiritual journey is to heal from past trauma. The more you traverse this healing path, you discover that this requires healing not only from this lifetime but past lifetimes too. We have all had many, many past lives – some good, some bad. We carry the trauma from these 'bad' past lives within our cells, within our energy. We are now being asked to clear this energy, these lifetimes and become as light and as clear a vessel as possible, moving forward. The energy from these past lives impacts our current life with differing intensities. When I do past life clearings for people, the trauma always resonates with them, and they can see where the energy has impacted them in this lifetime. I find that we don't need to clear the 'good' lifetimes as they don't impact our current life in a negative way. It's just the traumatic ones that tend to give us any issues! I have experienced lifetimes of abuse, torture, witch hunts ... none of them pleasant but all necessary to clear the energy from the person in this lifetime.

We also carry ancestral trauma in our energy. These are patterns that have been passed down through the generations through our DNA that are waiting to be healed. Ancestral trauma can be held within both the matriarchal and the patriarchal line and can influence our patterning in this lifetime. Epigenetics has proven how genes impact our behaviour and environment and how this is reversible. It isn't enough just to highlight and be aware of the energy pattern, it needs to be acknowledged by the ancestors so that they can feel heard. In my work, I find that ancestral clearing involves identifying the pattern/trauma/energy that has been passed down the generations in addition to speaking directly with the main ancestor where it all started (patient zero, I suppose).

Before getting lost in past lives and ancestral healing, healing from this lifetime is a good place to start. Healing yourself is an individual journey that can take you down some dark paths, but it is intended to always be of ultimate benefit as we begin to let go of our past and head towards our future a lot clearer, lighter and happier. I often get asked by people... how do you heal? How do you start letting go of what no longer serves you? When people start awakening to their spiritual path, they often have the desire to heal and let go but they don't know where to start or how to go about it.

There are various ways and different paths towards healing. My advice is to experiment and see which of the various methods that I suggest resonate and work for you. I find that at different times or for different topics, you will gravitate towards a different solution. So, just because a particular method worked well for releasing or clearing some energy or trauma, does not mean to say that you should always use this method. In the future, for a different aspect that has arisen to be healed, you may find that another method is more suitable. I like to think of the various ways as tools in my toolbox. I pull out the tool I consider most appropriate at the time.

Healing can take place on your own, and there are various methods which support this type of healing. Sometimes, being in your own space and allowing the emotions to rise without any kind of filter is very beneficial. Healing can also take place in a group setting (such as on a retreat) or during a 1-2-1 session with an experienced practitioner. The advantage to these types of healings is that you are being held in a supportive and loving environment which can help facilitate the trauma to be witnessed in a safe space. Sometimes, depending on the trauma, it can feel too scary and overwhelming to consider delving into those emotions on your own, so being with somebody who is experienced in facilitating these types of healings and holding space for the emotions to surface can be invaluable.

I don't wish to delve into all the science behind trauma and how it impacts us on a mental, physical and emotional level. I also do not wish to debate the various counselling theories on trauma. This is not what this chapter is about. This chapter is about giving practical advice from a spiritual perspective of having some understanding of trauma and how to go about releasing it. However, at some point during your healing journey, it may be appropriate that you seek medical or professional advice.

Whatever traumas you have experienced in life, regardless of the significance or size, it is stored in your body. When the trauma happens, it invokes a physical, mental and emotional response in your body which is then stored at a cellular level. The 'trauma' can cover a whole manner of situations and circumstances. It is not about deciding whether what has happened to you in life should constitute a 'trauma'. It is about accepting that things have happened to you during your life and having the desire to release the impact that they made. We like to judge ourselves, as well as others, in determining whether we should or should not label a particular incident as traumatic. Whatever has happened to you in your life is valid. It happened to you so therefore, it counts. It doesn't matter if other people have experienced far worse, or far less, than you – that is their journey. It is about being open and honest with your own journey and accepting that you have the right to consider certain events as traumatic. Some people's traumas have been completely horrific by any standards, such as being sold into a child trafficking ring. Another person's trauma might be being separated from their mother whilst out shopping. Both sets of traumas are equally valid and have caused a reaction in our bodies that has been frozen in time. To allow healthy healing of our bodies, these reactions/emotions need to be released. Starting with the energetic body and releasing on this level, allows it to eventually filter down to the physical body. Our physicality is made up of various bodies, the three main ones being the physical, mental and energetic bodies. Each impacts the other. If we do not address things at an energetic level, they eventually filter into the physical body – causing dis-ease.

Releasing the energy that is stuck in our bodies requires releasing emotions. Emotions are just energy in motion. Emotions are not good or bad, they just are. Expressing emotions is healthy and allows stuck energy to move. There is a whole scale of emotions such as fear, anger, guilt, pain and grief. All are valid. To me, a key part of healing is about allowing these emotions to be released and transmuted into something else. When releasing emotions, it is about having a trigger, something that allows you to connect with that emotion and then release it through your body.

I've listed a few methods below that are excellent tools to help trigger a release of emotions. Trial a few of them to see which works for you:

- *Music* - sometimes a particular piece of music has the power to shift energy within us and provide a release (this can be either slow or fast music).
- *Journalling* - writing your thoughts down onto paper is a great way to get things out of your head.
- *Fire ceremony* - using fire as a way to transmute energy is very powerful. Burning what you have written down can be very cathartic.
- *Crying* - always a good way to release emotions.
- *H'oponopono* - a Hawaiian forgiveness prayer which can be useful to shift energy.
- *Physical activity* - running, going to the gym or even punching a cushion can shift stuck emotions.
- *Meditation* - taking time to go within and be still can help identify how you are truly feeling, away from the busyness of everyday life, and;
- *Healing modalities* - such as breathwork, EFT, hypnosis, reiki and sound healing, for example, are all powerful ways in which we can be held in a safe space to allow big healing shifts.

Now, how do we start to release our trauma? Below are seven steps designed to assist you in releasing your trauma:

1. Choose a starting point. Start with the trauma that you are familiar with and go from there. There is no need to go looking for really deep traumas. Start with the things that you do know about, the things that you know are impacting your life right now. This may be to do with your childhood, relationships or work. Anything that comes to mind as an obvious incident or pattern that has impacted your life and has been instrumental in shaping you, but not necessarily in a good way, that is the place to start.
2. Allow your emotions. Once you have identified where you wish to start, the next step is to pick one of the above suggestions that you feel drawn to. A really good way to get started is to write down your thoughts and feelings on paper about the particular incident. Allow all of your emotions onto the paper – the anger, grief, sadness, frustration - whatever comes up, write it all down.
3. Do not filter or judge. Do not filter what you are thinking or feeling, let it all come through. This exercise is about allowing all of YOUR emotions to be released. It is not about having a balanced view and seeing it from all sides.
4. Acknowledge your trauma. This is about acknowledging what happened to you and to validate your emotions. It is what was true for you.
5. Allow yourself to express, not suppress. Part of the problem in having stuck emotions is that we are brought up in society to suppress our feelings and our true emotions. If we were allowed to express our emotions at the time, we would all be a lot healthier! Social

conditioning is only one reason why we do not express our emotions at the time but sometimes it would also not have been safe to. Allowing yourself to express your emotions using the written word provides a safe space that can be very freeing.

6. Do not re-absorb. Once you have expressed yourself on paper, do not read it back as you are then re-absorbing the energy.
7. Transmute the emotions. The final stage is about transmuting the energy that is on the paper and releasing it. There are various ways that you can do this from ripping it up and throwing it away, to cleansing it in water. My favourite way is to set fire to it! There is something very cathartic in watching all of that pain and anger that you have just released going up in smoke and being transmuted back to light.

As mentioned previously, this is a journey of healing layer after layer. Healing tends to be cyclic so a lot of the time, the same trauma comes back around again but you are then healing it on a different level. It is not because you didn't get it right the first time. There is no need to force healing. Things come to the surface to be witnessed and released at exactly the right time. Just be willing and open to start the process of coming back to your true self.

Another aspect of healing is about looking at your thought patterns and noticing what beliefs you have that no longer serve you. Your thoughts hold a lot of power and can impact the way that you feel and move through life. Your thoughts shape your mindset. Part of being able to consistently live in connection with the Divine is having an abundance mindset. It is about having an expansive and limitless mindset and not having constant fear-based thoughts and beliefs rolling around your head. The words that are in your head and that come out of your mouth carry a lot of weight and a lot of power. They carry significant intention, and they matter in what you manifest within your life. For example, if you are always telling yourself 'I never have enough money', or 'it's too expensive', then you predictably are never going to have enough money. Or, if you say to yourself 'I'm always late, I'm never on time,' then you can guarantee that you will always be late! Because that is your belief, your mindset, your programming that you have developed, over time, you will create a life that fulfills your belief. So, what you say to yourself, the words you choose and your beliefs, are very powerful because they carry such power and potent intention. It is very useful to regularly observe what you are saying. Observe what your beliefs are around money, around happiness, around love and around your career, for example. We always get our beliefs from somewhere. They have usually developed from someone saying something to us or something happening to us, possibly when we were a child. What we were told, and later on went to believe, has shaped our mindset and beliefs around that subject. You may have been impacted by people that you were surrounded by and have taken on board their beliefs and their patterning. Particularly when we are young, we have no filter, so we easily absorb and take on board other people's beliefs. Beliefs like:

- Money doesn't grow on trees.
- Life is a struggle.
- There is never enough time, or
- Nobody will ever love me.

It is worth taking some time to just observe what it is you say to yourself. Don't obsess over every single word you use, but gently introduce observing what you say about certain aspects of your life and what your beliefs are around certain things. Just take some time to establish what recurring thoughts and beliefs you have. Once you notice a pattern, you can then decide whether these beliefs are actually serving you, or whether you want to change them. A good place to start upgrading or shifting these old patterns is with affirmations. A simple starting point to create a more positive mindset is by saying daily positive affirmations. Choose an affirmation that is believable to you and within your reach. If you feel the affirmation is completely unattainable then it will lose its power and impact. For example, if the affirmation is about money, saying 'I am wealthy beyond my wildest dreams' might feel unachievable, so an affirmation such as 'I always have enough money for what I need' might resonate with you more and will prove more effective. You can build up to the first affirmation but always do this in stages.

Chapter 14

Quan Yin

Dearest friends please allow me to share my wisdom with you. Divine Living is achievable. It is achievable to you all. You need to have patience and to allow these teachings to embed within you. This takes time and practice. It is about showing up every day and being open to possibility. It is about having compassion with yourselves and each other, holding each other in deep compassion, with no judgement, and allowing yourself the opportunity and space to heal from traumas that have been locked within your energy field and lovingly be able to see yourself as nothing short of perfection. Yes, even now. You are whole and complete just as you are. There is no lack, nothing to attain, no destination to reach. It is an unfolding, a laying down of all the layers that do not serve you anymore but not viewing these layers as bad. They are perfection itself as all these layers are a part of you. They are a part of your story and are a part of what has got you to this point. Honour that. Honour each of these layers as you lay them down to rest. Acknowledge their part in your journey but know that it is time to lay them aside. They have served their purpose. They have served you well, but it is now time to lighten the load. It is okay to shed these layers that you are carrying. Recognise that although gifts in themselves, they have become burdens which are shielding you from your true essence. It is like watching a flower unfold and unfurl. Allow each petal to open, one at a time, discarding the petals that are no longer needed in order to be able to reveal the beautiful centre.

You have got this. You are stronger than you know, dear ones. You have already endured so much in this life and previous incarnations. Allow me to assist and help you to start to unfold. The process requires gentleness. A deep compassion towards yourself, for all that you have endured and an even deeper compassion for all those who have persecuted you. Forgiveness is the key to freedom. Forgiveness is the key to ultimate love - love for yourself and for everyone else, truly being able to understand that there is no separation. You are them and they are you. I am you and you are me. No separation, no judgement, just compassion, just love. Always love. Allow your heart to be open to this wisdom. Hear these gentle words. Allow them to soften your heart to all the perceived wrongs that you have suffered. Know, deep within, that there is no real suffering. At the centre, there is just peace. Allow me to guide you and help you achieve that peace, that inner stillness. It would be an honour to walk beside you. Know that this state can take just a moment to achieve but also know that in others this may take longer. Time is irrelevant. Do not judge yourself on the time it takes. This is counterproductive to your journey. Judgement puts walls up against love. Each time you feel judgement towards yourself or others, allow yourself to breathe and come back into a state of love and compassion. This state is achievable in each and every moment. Choose to make this the state that you wish to be in as much as you can. Start by consciously choosing this state until this becomes your default and your new normal in which to live. Know in your heart that you can do this. I send you all my love, compassion and wisdom, dear ones, and know that I am with you as you embark on this journey.

Chapter 15

Healing Journey with the Whales

Since my spiritual awakening, I have been on quite a roller coaster healing journey. I thought that I had cleared quite a lot of things, which I had, but I assumed that the majority of my work was done. Yet, I have found that there is always more healing to do.

The few months prior to departing for Tahiti were pretty intense. I felt energetically on my knees most of the time. Some mornings I would awake and feel that I hadn't had one minute of sleep, my eyes struggling to open and my body aching as if I had run a marathon overnight. I was going through healing cycle after healing cycle, clearing and releasing 'stuff' I didn't even know I had to release. It seemed a constant process and was happening during the night as well as during the day. I felt like I was literally crawling my way to my departure in September. At times, I felt that if what I was experiencing was just the preparation and build-up to connecting with the whale, then what on earth was it going to be like when I was actually there? I kept going with it and just allowing and releasing. I knew it was all enabling me to be as clear a channel as possible in preparation for my mission with Nagwal. My Divine team was amazing. They supported my energy to allow me to carry out my work with clients. I cut my client work down to a minimum to give me time to recover from my personal healing, and whenever I did work with a client, or hold my group monthly sessions, I could sense my guides stepping in and almost 'injecting' me with energy so I could be fully present and deliver the necessary service to whomever I was working with. As soon as my work was over, I would drop back down to experience whatever current energetic clearing I was in, usually immensely tired and disconnected from my current surroundings. I was regularly exhausted, and the healing was relentlessly present in my days.

It is very hard to put into words how intense this 'preparation' time was. Just when I thought I had completed the cycle of healing, another wave of past trauma would come to the surface for me to process, heal and let go. It was all-encompassing and omnipresent. During this time, there were a lot of past lives that came up for clearing – not one of them pleasant! I had the added 'bonus' of ancestral clearings required along both my matriarchal and patriarchal lines. I felt honoured (sort of!) to be clearing this energy that had been held onto by my ancestral bloodline, and I feel we have all brought our ancestral energies into our lifetime to finally clear and release. Typically, we heal our ancestral line, current life trauma and past lives over the course of our lifetime, I just seemed to be doing this work in a condensed timescale. I now know that I had the option and the free will of choice; I could have said 'no' at any stage of this healing and clearing, but it never occurred to me to do this. I just trusted that it was all being divinely guided, and I had the strength to get through whatever came up.

As my departure approached, I decided to confront my sea sickness issue and enlisted the help of an Emotional Freedom Technique

(EFT) practitioner, Vicki Powell, to see if I could get to the root cause of my motion sickness (go to www.kirstielilith.com/book-resources for further information). I had never tried EFT before and found it an excellent modality to navigate past all the surface issues and to deep dive into the core trauma and the reason why I struggled so much on boats. I had an inkling that my motion sickness related to pre-arriving on this planet, and this proved the case. During each session, we were able to explore paths that my conscious mind would never have thought of. As we discovered, my motion sickness was linked to my grief and sadness of leaving my family and planet to come to Earth. As mentioned previously, I am a Star Being originating from the planet Arcturus. My EFT practitioner was fabulous and never once judged or questioned the places we journeyed to during our sessions. I felt that we had some real breakthroughs. Due to my trip being so imminent, I had no opportunity to test whether I was healed of seasickness until I arrived in Tahiti. I had to have faith and trust that the sessions had created a huge impact. I just surrendered to what would be.

Just before I was about to leave on my trip, I was approached by numerous ocean mammals saying that they would be energetically supporting me while in Tahiti and I needed to energetically connect with them. From orcas to pods of dolphins, these offers of energetic support flooded in. Just like the vision that Nagwal had initially shared with me, the other species were connecting and uniting together for the greater good. It was very humbling. I was blown away by how much support I was starting to get prior to even departing and to me, it just highlighted the magnitude of what Nagwal and I were attempting to do.

PART FIVE

PLAYING SMALL

Chapter 16

Playing Small

> *I am not afraid.*
>
> *I was born to do this.*
>
> — Joan of Arc

Often, we think that playing small is the right thing to do - for us and for others. Playing small is about being less than you actually are. It is about pretending that you're less clever, less pretty, less well-off, less spiritual or less talented than you actually are. These are just a few examples of how we can play small in our lives. I recall being in my corporate job and knowing that what my boss said was wrong, but I didn't want to speak up for fear of making him look bad. We do it to fit in and to make other people feel more comfortable. We think that if we don't stand out and instead try to make ourselves the same as everyone else, we will be liked, we will be accepted and it will make us feel more 'normal'. NO. The time for playing small is over. Diminishing who you are to make others feel more comfortable is not beneficial for you or them. It does neither party justice. It prevents both sides from expanding, developing and growing.

Keeping safe and not rocking the boat does not allow you to expand and reach your full potential. Dumbing down who you actually are is never the answer. Nobody likes to be the odd one out in the crowd, because it goes against the law of nature: the animal that is different from all the others usually ends up as prey for a predator. It is instinct and survival behaviour to want to fit in. By pretending to be less than you actually are, you may initially make the other person feel less threatened and more comfortable around you, but in the long run, it doesn't help either one of you. It stunts both of your soul's growth and your ability to expand into who you truly are.

Now is the time to stop playing small. Stop trying to shrink your light and hide your true magnificence just to feel more accepted and more like everyone else. In reality, it doesn't actually work. At some level, people see through the guise. They instinctively know that you are different and pretending to be someone that you're not. Accepting that you are different from others is a massive step. Accepting that it is okay to be different means that you can start accepting yourself more fully. You are different. Everyone is. We are all unique. We are all imperfectly perfect and yet we spend so much of our lives trying to be the same as everyone else. This stops now. Make that conscious decision to stop trying to dim your light, your true nature and your abilities to try and fit in with others. Make the decision to shine your light as brightly as you possibly can, to be the most expansive version of yourself and to live a life with no limits, no glass ceiling. Understand that if we are all unique, comparing ourselves to somebody else is actually pointless. It's like comparing apples to oranges. How could someone else be able to define whether we have reached the goal of being the very best version of ourselves by judging ourselves by another's standards? It's a futile exercise because their best version, their limit and their ceiling are completely different to yours.

It is about following your own path, your own authentic journey, and fully embracing the fact that you are completely unique. You are here to shine your inner light as brightly as possible and to keep on shining as you expand. Expand more and continue expanding until you feel you have reached your full potential. At that point, you could take a pause, observe and then congratulate yourself on how far you have come and how far you have grown. Hopefully, at this point, you will also realise that there are no limits in this life, only the ones we place on ourselves or allow others to place on us and you will take another breath and continue to expand and shine even brighter. We set our own limitations. When we allow ourselves to fully surrender to the Divine and to let go, that is when the magic happens.

When we play small, it is our ego trying to keep us safe. What if we were able to set aside our own limiting beliefs, our own fears and our self-doubts? What if we just let go of all that, fully surrendered and just allowed? If we broke through our own glass ceiling, what we could potentially achieve could be extraordinary.

Chapter 17

Lilith

Greetings my dear brothers and sisters. Divine Living is about balance. It is the balance of all parts of yourself. The balance between the light and the dark, the good and the bad, the left and the right, the feminine and the masculine. It is about achieving balance within you and also without. When you are able to live in balance both in your inner and outer world, you are able to connect with your stillpoint – the silence within, that inner peace. Everything starts to make sense and have meaning. A big part of this is valuing yourself. Recognise how unique and amazing you are, just as you are, the complete perfection in all of you, without the need or desire to fit in, to be liked, to be accepted. Know that you are perfect just as you are. So often, I witness your need to gain approval, to gain acceptance, to feel 'normal' and to feel like you belong. I see how you shrink your magnificent self to accommodate another person in your life, in order for them to feel more than. I see how you play small so as not to rock the boat, to make others feel comfortable, to make yourself feel comfortable, to delude yourself and others that this is who you are, that this is all of who you are. Keeping yourself as you currently are is not expansive. It is not growth; it is not progression. Keeping the status quo for whatever limiting reason is just that – limiting. Enough! Life is about expansion, it is about joy, it is about love. It is about fully experiencing everything, knowing that you are limitless. There is so much possibility with each and every one of you. It is about recognising this and making the decision to stop limiting yourself, to release the shackles that you, others and society as a whole have placed upon you, by allowing all parts of yourself to be witnessed and accepted. To allow the good and the bad, the dark and the light to take their rightful place together again, side-by-side. No more hiding, no more presenting only the side of you which you consider acceptable. No more being suppressed. No more playing the good girl, the good boy, the dutiful and the meek. It is about recognising the power within you – that true essence, your divinity, your birthright, your right to be truly seen in all your radiance. This is not selfish – this is self-love.

Heal from all the generations and centuries of suppression, of being held down and being bound by society's rules. Release these shackles now and break free. Decide today that no more will you conform to fit in. Decide that you will forge your own future, your own path, where you will allow your inner light to be your compass, your guidance system. Allow yourself to experience the inner truth. You are a limitless being, stop placing limits on yourself, stop allowing others to place limits on you. Be free and fly, dear ones! Be who you came here to be. Claim your power back. Claim your power back from others where you have allowed them to take it. Give away your power no more. Recognise that this does not serve you or them. Place no blame or judgement, just observe your present situation and witness where you have relinquished your power. Observe that they have not taken this from you; you have given this away. A big part of reclaiming your power is to recognise that it is you, and only you, that can give away your power. It is therefore you, and only you, that can take it back again. Reclaim your power with grace, recognise the sovereign being that you are and collect the parts of yourself that you have handed over to others. To be fully sovereign you need to be whole, to be balanced, to be fully accepting, to not be pulled off-balance by the people in your life, to not play games and be less than to make others feel comfortable. It is safe to be who you are, it is safe to allow others to see who you are. It is time to claim your power, to claim your light, your true sovereignty and to fully recognise the magnificent being of divine light that you are. Decide today that you will live in the shadow no more. Step into the light, dear ones – it is time.

Chapter 18

Stop Playing Small

As I said previously, the level of support from both humans and my spirit guides that I received prior to my trip was phenomenal and it continued to escalate the closer I drew to flying to Tahiti. I had various 'beings' coming in constantly, offering their support and assistance for this imminent trip. At times, I felt quite overwhelmed and the enormity of what I was attempting to accomplish grew the closer I got to my departure. One such helper started off as a nuisance when a huge bug flew into my house and took up residence in the corner of one of my rooms. I had never seen a bug this huge that also had wings! As it remained with me in the house for a couple of days, unwilling to leave, I knew it had come to impart an important spiritual message to me. I decided to tune into this bug's message and this flying insect dropped this bombshell: Counter to what I had been telling myself, this bug stated clearly and without a doubt, that there were no others that would be, nor could be, carrying out this 'mission'. The entire work was left to be completed by me, and me alone. At this point, I dropped to my knees sobbing on my bedroom floor and unable to breathe properly for many minutes. The beautiful construct that I had built over the months to protect myself from this weight of responsibility shattered in an instant. The huge pressure and enormity of what I was going to do hit me like a sledgehammer.

Why me?

What if I failed?

What if I couldn't do it?

What if I was not enough?

All those doubting questions rose to the surface. The years of me not stepping into my own power and owning the space that I was capable of completing such a mammoth task were staring right back at me in this one simple message. I had been playing small, keeping myself safe and had avoided any opportunity to be visible!

My limiting beliefs went into overdrive, resulting in questioning what on earth the Divine were thinking when they chose me for this mission. Surely, there must be thousands of other people much better qualified than me to do this. I started berating my higher self (yet again!) for volunteering and getting me into this mess!

I'd like to share at this point that I always visualise my higher self as an excitable little girl with her hand permanently raised in the air, jumping up and down in excitement squealing 'Pick me, pick me!' In my mind, I keep having the same conversation with her: 'Put your hand down! STOP volunteering us for stuff! We have enough going on!' And this was yet another one of those moments.

This beautiful flying bug also triggered a lot of fear in me (I'm not that keen on insects and bugs at the best of times, let alone one that seemed more at home in the laboratory of a Marvel movie!) All my carefully constructed webs of delusion and subterfuge, tenderly built over years to keep myself safe, came crashing down. I was face-to-face with multiple of my fears: The fear of being truly seen, the fear of owning who I am, and the fear of owning my light and my power. This bug brought up all of those fears in its one shocking statement – fears that I had to acknowledge and own. As Marianne Williamson beautifully wrote:

> ‘Our deepest fear is not that we are inadequate. Our deepest fear is that we are powerful beyond measure. It is our light, not our darkness, that most frightens us.’

Yet again, I had a lot to process and release as I needed to let go of the overwhelm and start surrendering to what would be. I had to completely let go of my doubts, fears and limiting beliefs and put my trust in the divine plan. I did feel, at times, like I was hanging onto the edge of a cliff just by my fingernails. It was not easy to just keep breathing and letting go of all my fears and overwhelm while desperately grasping onto the last tatters of what I saw as my sanity and security. My guides continued to have unshakable faith in me though, even when I didn’t. It helped when, in a healing session with a powerful intuitive channel, I was given the guidance that there was nothing to fear, it was already done. I had already achieved what was necessary. I was shown in this space of ‘NOW’ – time is not linear and is an illusion and that there is only ever the ‘now’… and in this space, my work in Tahiti was already done. I did not fail. The relief that I felt was amazing and those words immediately helped dispel any lingering doubt and overwhelm.

Part Six

FEAR

Chapter 19

Fear

> *F.E.A.R*
>
> *has two meanings:*
>
> *Forget Everything and Run*
>
> *or*
>
> *Face Everything and Rise*
>
> *The choice is yours.*
>
> — Zig Ziglar

Fear is when the body is held rigid in that freeze stage just between fight or flight. It is when the body or mind is unable to make a decision, unable to focus and decide which choice to make. Fear leads to us acting as a victim and not from the point of view of a predator or someone in control. Fear causes you to act irrationally and without consequences. It can cause irrational behaviour as well as negative physiological effects on the body –

accelerated breathing, increased heart rate, exhaustion, adrenaline rushing through your body, a cold dread at the pit of your stomach. Fear is not a nice situation to be in, and not the ideal state to be acting from. When we are in the fear response, we let that be the dominant trait. We lose connection to ourselves and to who we really are. When we are acting from a fear response, we automatically lose our connection to love. Fear is at the opposite end of the spectrum to love. We can either act from fear or from love. We have this choice – always. Fear, as well as a physiological response, can also be a programmed response. It can be the way we've always responded to situations. It can be our default. It can be from how we have been brought up, witnessing how our parents and friends respond. We have learnt behaviours of how to respond to certain situations from a fear point of view. It can sometimes feel like the easiest option. It is the less expansive route, the one that appears easiest, the one with less hardship and the point of view that takes the least amount of courage.

Acting from a place of fear is limiting. Acting from a place of love is expansive.

But choosing expansive can feel scary because it is stepping into the unknown. Acting from a place of fear can be familiar, even reassuring in a way. It's the way you've always responded, this way will keep you safe, keep you small. But it is time to stop playing small. It's time to stop fitting into others' ideals of who you should be or who you shouldn't be. It is time to break free of the constraints that fear places on us. It may feel safe, but it is slowly suffocating you. It is restricting you. It is squeezing the life out of you. It is time to breathe properly. It is time to choose to operate from a place of love, a place of expansiveness, a place of non-restriction. In every moment you can choose to operate from a place of love or fear. It is easy to determine which response you are choosing by how you are feeling.

Does it make you feel constricted, small and safe?

OR

Does it make you feel challenged, expansive and unrestricted?

Fear can show up in many different ways. It is not just a physical reaction to a situation. There is fear of failure and fear of success, fear of judgement or fear of rejection. There is even the fear of making a decision. Sometimes the pain of not making a decision or acting on something is worse than the fear itself.

FEAR v LOVE. There is always a choice in where we operate from. It's time to stop playing small. True Divine Living is about recognising that we do have a choice in how we act. It is about taking responsibility for ourselves and deciding that we can either be frozen and immobilised by life, or we can choose to step off the proverbial cliff and see where life takes us. If we choose this latter option, then we open ourselves to the possibility of learning to fly!

Chapter 20

Isis

Living in connection with the Divine is what I would wish for everyone. It is my dream, the ultimate way to be living. Many of you who are reading these words have lived this way many times before. You understand, at soul level, what it feels like. Allow yourself to start remembering. Allow your soul to lead the way. It is like a feeling of coming home to yourself. It is the only way to be, living in peace, love and harmony, devoid of fear and choosing love over fear in every moment. There is so much fear on your planet and it causes you to contract. Fear is such a dense energy; it stifles the breath. It prevents true expansion, in this breath, in this body and in the soul. Fear prevents you from having freedom. When you live in harmony with the Divine, it is true freedom. There is an expansion of joy in every moment. There is a freedom of expression, a freedom of being connected to your true self, your powerful self – to be able to stand in your own power, in your light, to radiate this from every cell in your body – pure freedom and bliss. This state comes from the absence of fear, it comes from knowing that everything is in divine order. There is a purpose and a reason for everything. There is just an inner knowing that everything is okay, everything is unfolding just as it is meant to in perfect divine timing. It is just a matter of surrendering in each and every moment and allowing this to happen. It is a simple process to align yourself to this state. It is remembering how that causes the challenge. So, keep trying to attain this state, dear ones. It will become more natural to you. You will be able to feel when you attain this state. Initially, it will only be for a short time and then you will move out of alignment and back into your more normal, fear-based living. As you continue to practise, it will become easier and will become your most natural way of being. It will become the only way for you to be. Any other state will feel abrasive and uncomfortable. You will desire that peace and sense of connectedness that you only achieve when in true alignment with the Divine. Seek this alignment, this state, for this is where true happiness and true contentment are found. This is the ultimate goal for your incarnation on Earth, this being connected to your true self, allowing the Divine to express itself in true perfection through you. Some of you are able to reach this state already, others are still shrouded in fear and illusion. This fog needs to be cleared before any lasting alignment can be forged. When you still primarily operate from a fear-based system, the moments of connecting with the Divine are fleeting. You just catch glimpses. The more the fear is lifted, the longer you are able to maintain this state of joy and peace. Do not fall into judgement of where you are, this is allowing the ego to control you and keep you in a fear mentality. A love focus has no need for the ego, for keeping you safe, keeping you small. Love is truly expansive and knows that you are always safe, there is always enough and there is no need to doubt. Everything is just as it needs to be. Follow my guidance, follow my light, my dear children. Allow me to offer my support and guide you, once again, to remembering your true selves, to once again align yourself to the only true power – the power within. Of All That Is. And so, it is.

Chapter 21

The Retreat Begins!

I will never forget setting off for Tahiti. As I sat down in my aircraft seat, Nagwal came to me and said, 'It is time to dance, you and I'. Big gulp.

It was a long and tiring journey, covering thousands of miles and multiple layovers. When I was recuperating on one such stop in Papeete, Tahiti, I was guided to carry out a water ceremony on the powerful 9/9 portal. Fortunately, this was the only spiritual work I was guided to do, so I could spend the rest of my time in solitude, grounding myself and reflecting on the next stage of my journey.

The retreat itself was on the stunning island of Moorea, the island next to Tahiti. The energy of the island was so heart-centred that I was instantly engulfed in a blanket of love that radiated from the land. The island is said to be linked to the Egyptian pyramids and the Isles of Avalon and I could certainly feel that ancient wisdom as I connected with the island. The resort where we were staying was amazing, the self-contained bungalows were far plusher than I had envisaged, and the decking looked out onto the mountains of Moorea. My bungalow was just a short walk to the idyllic white sand beach and teal blue ocean I had only ever dreamed of. I was, yet again, asked to perform another water ceremony. After setting the intention of my work here with the whales, ocean and the land, I took my sacred water and mixed it with the Pacific Ocean. I entered the sea and fully anchored my energy into this space.

That afternoon was the first time I would meet the retreat group. There were twelve beautiful souls in total, of which ten were participants, as well as Celeste, the woman running the retreat, and her assistant. As I discovered, all the other participants had been on previous retreats with Celeste. They had all been swimming with whales or dolphins for many years, so for some of the participants, it was a friendly reunion. After the initial introductions, the assistant started to give us some information about what we were going to encounter over the next couple of weeks. This is when reality started sinking in of what I had actually signed myself up for.

'Remember that there are ten shark breeds that regularly frequent these waters, and only the White Tip Reef shark is safe to approach. Be particularly careful of Oceanic White Tips, Black Tips, Tiger sharks and Hammerheads...'

She had my undivided attention as I reached for some water to moisten my dry mouth.

As I found out over the next couple of weeks, she was not into over-dramatics and exaggerations. We encountered sharks every single day while we were in the ocean. This real threat of sharks was something that she repeated every single day on the boat before we got into the water. It was something that I could never forget and trying desperately to keep my face calm and composed on that Sunday afternoon, while my stomach was clenched in stone-cold fear and my brain rapidly tried to process the full horror of what my ears were absorbing would forever stay with me. At this point, I silently sent out a prayer to anyone that would listen.... 'HELP ME!'... God, a random stranger... anyone really, I wasn't picky, I just wanted some reassurance that I wasn't about to die!

I hadn't anticipated this little issue of navigating sharks in the same water as me. Sure, I knew that I was going to be in the ocean, but to swim with whales... only whales. It hadn't crossed my mind that there would be other critters swimming in the ocean too! Up to this point, I thought my biggest concern was going to be the fact that there was no toilet on the boat (I have a very small bladder!) This fact alone would normally have sent me into a mini panic. Also, the boat was a lot smaller than I had anticipated. I hadn't expected a huge boat, but I had expected it to be big enough to house a small toilet! Also, I quickly registered that a small boat would mean that we would be more at the mercy of the ocean. The picture in my mind of a really small boat on a big choppy ocean instantly brought to the forefront my seasickness. Could this day get any worse?

It most certainly could. I thought the tiny boat, no toilet and the prospect of being bitten by sharks was the low point but no, there was more. As the introduction continued, the assistant explained the mechanics of how we would swim with the whales. Apparently, so as not to disturb the whales, we would be dropped quite a distance from them and then we would need to swim (sometimes up to a mile) to be with them. She emphasised the deep water and strong currents that we would encounter. Definitely not for the fainthearted. At this point I surveyed the room, assessing my fellow swimmers with their extensive ocean swimming experience and model-like bodies. I became painfully aware of my own, very unfit, couch potato body with zero ocean-swimming experience. My naive assumption had been that we would gently climb down a ladder into the water right next to the whales and then float on the water, observing them in their natural habitat and eventually climb back on board the boat. Oh, the blissful ignorance of those rose-coloured spectacles... where were they now? While processing the stark reality of what I had signed up for, I got paler and paler as the physical challenges of what I was to embark on really hit home. It also made me very aware of my own ignorance and lack of fore-thought. All the physical aspects of what I could or would encounter had never entered my head. I had blissfully arrived in Moorea, following instructions from a whale, without ANY consideration for the actual reality.

After the introduction, I didn't sleep much before our first boat outing. The thought of what I was going to encounter terrified me and being perfectly honest, I spent most of that night in tears. Having witnessed my own and others' healing journeys, I find it really interesting to look at the things that trigger us. Normally, the lack of toilet facilities for several hours would send me into a hysterical frenzy. For that night, this typically large issue didn't even register. A logical assumption on the fear scale would be the impending doom of swimming with sharks would far exceed any bathroom break requirement. You would have thought that the shark factor was what kept me awake and crying into my pillow until the wee small hours, but, oh no, the sharks didn't even come into the equation. Interestingly, what I was triggered by, to the point of emotional paralysis, was FEAR OF JUDGEMENT. I was afraid of being the weakest link in the group. I was afraid of letting the others down, of being judged by them, of not physically being capable of achieving what I had come here to achieve. I was afraid of my body letting me down, and that I would fail. All these fears rose to the surface to engulf me and were made visible for me to either drown under them or process them. The weight of responsibility that I felt over not being enough came crashing down on me to deal with that night. It was a very long night as all these judgements swirled around my head. Gradually, as I released each layer of judgement with the therapeutic steps of healing, I took another step closer towards complete acceptance and the embodiment of my true self.

As a side note, upon my return to the UK, I was curious to discover that each and every person in my close circle of friends had experienced swimming in the ocean. In the lead-up to my going on this retreat, not one of them felt guided to share this piece of information with me or to enlighten me on what I would encounter while swimming with the whales. As I shared my ordeal with them, every one of my friends admitted that they knew of the physical challenges that I would face and how tough it was going to be. I could understand if one of my friends hadn't received guidance to support me or they had not felt guided to share, but ALL of them? I knew at this point that their silence in the matter of ocean swimming and preparing for it was also divinely guided. They were not meant to share their knowledge and experience with me. If I had known back then what I now know, I would definitely have gone to the gym and got fitter. I would definitely have practised swimming in the ocean and using my snorkel gear. I would have been more 'prepared', I would have felt more in 'control'. But if I had prepared, I wouldn't have had the immense shock and subsequent triggers, and I wouldn't have seen the self-judgement that I was still carrying that needed healing. I find it fascinating how things are divinely orchestrated to allow these opportunities to come to the surface. All we need to do is to allow.

Chapter 22

Vulnerability

> *Be weird.*
>
> *Be random.*
>
> *Be who you are.*
>
> *Because you never know who*
>
> *Would love the person you hide.*
>
> — *C S Lewis*

Allowing yourself to be vulnerable, truly vulnerable, is probably one of the hardest things to do. It goes against our fundamental DNA and our survival instincts. We are hard-wired to protect ourselves and to not show weakness. Survival of the fittest and all that! But part of successfully being able to live in conjunction with the Divine and to be truly free is to be able to allow yourself to be vulnerable, to really be able to let others see the real you – warts and all; to be able to expose your soft underbelly and to give people the opportunity to hurt you. It's important to let people in close enough to be able to truly hurt you because you are also allowing them and yourself the opportunity to love and be loved. You open yourself up to wondrous possibilities and experience love for who you authentically are. Vulnerability allows you the freedom of just being – no game playing and no holding on out of fear-based reactions, just allowing yourself to be in the stream of pure love. It is only from this state of pure love that you can finally be free. This is the core, the essence of being able to live and connect with your divinity. It is about being able to live from this place of complete vulnerability. For your heart to be so open and to live from a place of purity - some may call it unconditional love. Total unconditional love for both yourself and others.

Does this sound impossible? Maybe. Is it achievable? You can only find out if you start taking those steps to allow all those deeply constructed walls of protection to start collapsing, one brick at a time. Are you ready to hold my hand and take the first step? It is only by allowing ourselves to step out of the shadow that we can be truly seen.

Being vulnerable takes practice. It takes time to observe and notice the walls that we put up around ourselves to keep us safe and protected. But they also keep others out and they keep us locked in. In order to remove the wall, the bricks need to come down, one brick at a time. This is a job that only you can do. Letting go of your defence mechanisms is not easy, but it is achievable. Start small. Start with a particular person in your life and then move on to another and then another.

Top tips for being vulnerable:

- Accept help. You may be used to doing everything yourself but allowing someone to help and offer assistance gives you the opportunity to be vulnerable.
- Don't hide your emotions. Allow others to see the full range of your emotions – cry, rant or laugh loudly in public, for example.
- Don't pretend everything is okay. Don't plaster a smile on your face and pretend that everything is okay – be real.
- It's okay to show weakness. We think we need to be strong all the time – it's okay to let people see our weaknesses.

Once you make the decision to be vulnerable, life will always find ways and situations where you can test being vulnerable. It will not always be a situation that you would choose but it will provide you with an invaluable opportunity to allow yourself to be open and come from a place of love. For example, you might be waiting for the bus and realise that you left your wallet at home. Do you leave the queue and start to walk the long journey ahead of you rather than take the bus or do you allow yourself to be vulnerable and ask for help from one of your fellow passengers?

Just keep breathing and know that you can do this.

Chapter 23

Here's to Being Vulnerable!

I was given an ideal opportunity to allow myself to be vulnerable. It was definitely a situation that I would have avoided had I the choice, yet, by passing through this experience, I not only survived, but I also developed a greater understanding of being vulnerable.

The morning of my first boat trip to meet the whales arrived, and I had barely slept the night before. As I nervously prepared myself for the day ahead, I tentatively ate two dried crackers along with seasickness pills for my breakfast. I was praying that my EFT sessions had worked, and I was cured of seasickness, but I hadn't tested whether this was a reality or my misplaced hopes. Today might, or might not, be my first-ever boat outing without being violently sick. So, with my concern weighing heavily on my mind, I tried to find some element of the trip that I was confident about. There was nothing. The physical challenge of swimming, swimming in deep water and deep water that also had sharks in it all created a space of utmost terror for me.

Blindly going through my daily routine, I can barely remember how I got to the harbour or when I boarded the boat. I was operating on autopilot. The ocean was relatively calm as we headed out into the 'deep blue' to go looking for our beloved whales, and with this smooth trip, the knot of fear in my belly slowly loosened. We did not have to wait long until the first whale sighting occurred... it was like they had been waiting for us! We came across a couple of males, and it was breathtaking to see these beautiful creatures in the ocean; to be able to witness as they came to the surface to breathe and to see the telltale spray of mist before they dove back down into the ocean, and to experience the final magical sight of their tails, called flukes, rising out of the water before they disappeared below. The whales changed their direction. They started swimming straight towards us and stopped right next to the boat. Tuning into Nagwal, he said that it was the whales welcoming me and validation of the work that I was about to do. I was so humbled that I received so much validation from the whales with this unexpected and unusual welcome. I was so grateful to them for this seemingly simple action because I had many an occasion to doubt what I was doing, especially when my spiritual work took me to the edge of crazy!

Seeing these beautiful whales swim so close to the side and underneath our boat, without even creating a wave or ripple was an incredible sight. Still in the boat, we followed these male whales until they finally slowed down and settled enough for us to start preparing to enter the water and swim with them.

I have no idea why the facilitator waited until this moment to ask four seemingly simple questions, yet my answers rocked the boat more than any wave ever could!

'Kirstie, have you ever been swimming with whales before?'

'No.'

'Okay, have you been swimming with dolphins before?'

'No.'

There was a pause as Celeste, the facilitator, and the group processed this new piece of information. The helpful assistant interjected, trying to remove the awkward silence that we were all sitting in, 'But you have been swimming in the ocean before though, haven't you?'

'No.'

I was suddenly aware of the immense silence surrounding me, and the people on the boat. Glancing up, I was met with every single person staring intently at me. I could feel the tension rising and the looks of consternation passing between each other.

'But you have snorkelled before?' the assistant asked, nervously.

There was no point in dragging out the immense discomfort I was feeling, so answered a simple 'No'.

I didn't see any value to be added by admitting that I hadn't even tried on the snorkel gear that I rush-purchased from a shop en route to the airport last week.

I didn't need to be psychic to be able to read everyone's mind on the boat at this point. To a greater or lesser degree, they were thinking 'What idiot flies halfway around the world to swim with whales and has never even been swimming in the ocean before?' That idiot would be me! Thank goodness no one chose to ask at that point why I was actually there because I think that the silence following that answer would have been even more stark!

The worst critic of them all was me. I was judging myself harshly. I felt really overwhelmed with the weight of my own stupidity. A stark realisation came to mind that there was a very thin line between bravery and stupidity, and I had well and truly jumped with both feet into the 'stupid' side. My complete lack of experience or preparation was very apparent to every single person on this boat.

Without a word being muttered, Celeste got up. Her assistant followed and went to have a hushed conversation with the boat Captain and swim guide. The regular glances over to me were a constant reminder of the subject of this intense conversation. Without a word ushered, they passed me a small inflatable buoy, which seemed to be the signal to wordlessly say that I was allowed to enter the water. Looking at the small, blue device, no larger than a shoe box, I did wonder how on earth this float would help me in the water, but I clung onto it as if it contained the key to the universe! And, over the next couple of weeks, this little float became my comfort blanket for the trip, and I would not enter the water without it!

That first time entering the water was a bit of a blur. I remember that there was not a lot of swimming involved (thank goodness!) and the sea was fairly calm. As I slid down the side of the boat, I entered the water with a big splash and my whole body was submerged, including my snorkel. I bobbed to the surface frantically spitting out the salt water that was now in my mouth. I couldn't see very well due to my mask taking on water, but I was still clutching my blue float! Celeste helped me adjust my mask, so it was properly sealed and not cutting off the circulation to my ears anymore. All of this initial mayhem helped take my focus off where I actually was - in the ocean with miles of dark sea water below me with goodness knows what critters lurking there. My heart hammered in my chest the whole of that first swim as I continued to gasp for air. I hadn't anticipated how challenging using fins would be. It looks so natural when you see people using them in films! That first swim, they spent most of the time out of the water ineffectively splashing around as I tried to get myself to where the whales were. When we were floating on the surface with our heads in the water, I could vaguely make out a whale swimming below us but they were far beneath me so I couldn't discern what whale I was looking at. It didn't help that I am short-sighted and wear glasses, so seeing whales at a distance in the ocean with no glasses on was not my forte... luckily for me, they are quite large! My focus on that first outing was mainly spent on controlling my breathing to a steady and calm pace and overcoming my fear of deep water.

It was a huge relief to finally climb up the metal ladders and make it back onto the boat. Adrenalin was coursing through my veins and my whole body was shaking as it processed what had just happened. My heart expanded with joy and the sheer elation of what I had accomplished. I had swum in the ocean with whales and sharks – and I survived! I had conquered my fear and I had done it. Still reeling from all these emotions, another very familiar feeling started to wash over me. Oh god, I'd forgotten about the seasickness! The boat was tiny so there was no privacy and no bathroom to throw up in. Desperately looking around, I realised that the only option was to lean over the side of the boat and throw up into the pristine blue ocean I had moments before been swimming in. The two dried crackers I ate for breakfast were lost straight away, yet just because my stomach was empty didn't mean I stopped retching and heaving. It was relentless. My heaving didn't stop for the majority of the boat trip back, the longest three hours of my life. It was only when I staggered off the boat that I stopped vomiting and started feeling anywhere close to normal. Allowing myself to be vulnerable about my seasickness was the only option.

On about the tenth time of retching over the side of the boat, and positive I'd lost practically all of my stomach lining by this point, I made a decision. I categorically stated *I hate you Nagwal!* (not my finest moment!) and then I vowed to never step foot on this boat, or any other boat for the rest of my life, with a final nail in the coffin stating that Nagwal could find some other idiot to complete this mission. The thought of going through the immense vomiting every day for the next two weeks filled me with dread and I refused to consider doing it. The universe would just have to find someone else. I QUIT.

Desperately searching for anything to help reduce the nausea, I decided to try lying flat on the boat. Everything else had failed, so it was worth giving it a go. I was vaguely aware that the others had gone back into the ocean when the boat stopped again but I had no energy to lift my head to see what was going on. My whole body was shaking, and I was too preoccupied with trying to stop being sick to care about anything else. Amazingly enough, lying flat did work. I stopped throwing up and started to feel less sick. When I finally stopped shaking, I spent a moment tuning into the whales that were close to us. It was a beautiful and magical experience to be able to connect with these beings that were just right under the boat. To be so close to them physically and to feel their intense but calm energy filled me with such gratitude.

Eventually, it was time to return to shore and we started heading back inland until we reached a lagoon. As I raised my head and peered over the side of the boat to see why we had stopped, in the teal-blue shallow water I could see that there were dozens of sharks and manta rays swimming around. Even though it was the last thing I felt like doing, I was advised that it would be good for me to go into the water to practise using my fins. Once I got over the concern of being surrounded by sharks, (amazing that in just one day I went from 'petrified' to 'curious' about swimming with the sharks!) I was able to focus on trying to use my fins in some sort of useful way. Once I realised that I needed to use my hips to control the fins, my swimming action became less clunky and slightly more coordinated. I loved swimming with the rays as they glided past me with only inches to spare. I couldn't quite stop the thought entering my head though that Steve Irwin had been killed by a manta ray. Not helpful at this point!

To say I was mightily relieved when we finally ended up on dry land is an understatement. I refrained from throwing myself prostate onto the pier and kissing the solid ground (I decided it seemed a little over dramatic as I'd already embarrassed myself enough for one day). I was exhausted and after a hot shower and food, I fell into a deep sleep. I was still resolved that I was not going back onto the boat to repeat the horrendous ordeal of the morning. I decided I would share my decision with the rest of the group the following morning. During the night, I reflected on the day and decided I was completely within my right to not go back onto the boat as I had total free will as a human. As soon as that statement passed through my mind, something just clicked into place. A couple of years back, I had made the decision to hand my life over to the Divine and from that point on I have chosen to follow divine will over my own free will. At that moment, I realised that I would indeed be going back on the boat in the morning and also every single day after that until the end of the retreat, even if it meant that I was violently sick every single day. It is so interesting how a moment of clarity can allow everything to fall into place. At that moment I received my clarity and a new sense of purpose that

I wouldn't let Nagwal down and I would continue to do all that he asked. I didn't consider myself a martyr or a hero (a bit of an idiot maybe), I was just resolved to complete my divine mission... no matter what.

After my revelation during the night, I made my way back onto the boat with slightly less trepidation than the day before. Only slightly, I might add, as despite my resolve to complete this mission, I still had the fear of being in the ocean and the seasickness to contend with. With the memory of being violently sick the day before still fresh in my mind, we made our way out into the deep ocean looking for whales. I focused on my breath to ground my energy, to bring me back into my body and keep myself calm. All I actually wanted to do was to throw myself into the water and frantically swim back towards the now disappearing shoreline. Oh... and cry! My stomach started to swirl in dread. The other retreat members chatted companionably amongst themselves as I stared studiously ahead in the direction we were going, as if sheer will alone would keep the contents of my stomach where they were. I was sufficiently distracted though when we came across a mummy whale with her calf. As we were observing them both, the mummy whale rolled over onto her belly and raised her pectoral fin, right in front of our boat. My whale experts on the boat said that they had never seen a mummy whale act in this way before.

I tuned into her while I was watching this touching display, and she shared the following:

> *'Humans live too much in their heads, it is important that they start dropping their focus into their hearts and living from this space. They also need to allow themselves to be vulnerable – like I am doing now. And to know that it's safe to be vulnerable. Part of the wounded masculine energy on earth is that unwillingness to be vulnerable.'*

I thought this was a beautifully inspiring message from her as she demonstrated this message by allowing herself and her calf to be completely exposed and vulnerable in front of us. It is so rare for wild animals to display such behaviour as they are naturally defensive when around predators, such as ourselves.

Part Seven

SURRENDER

Chapter 24

Surrender

> *You'll never learn to fly.*
>
> *If you can't let go.*
>
> — *Unknown*

To fully allow and surrender seems so easy to say but how do we do it? If we have grown up in an environment where it was not safe to do so, or we were not shown or given a blueprint of how to do this, how do we actually know? People can advise us to 'just surrender', but what does that actually entail?

What does surrendering mean? To me, surrendering is a process of discovering how to open yourself up more and more, like peeling layers of an onion. To fully surrender and let go is about allowing yourself to be vulnerable. Being vulnerable with ourselves seems a huge task in itself, but being vulnerable in front of others is a whole different ball game. Again, this is all a step-by-step process. Be easy on yourself. Being able to let go and fully surrender takes time to master.

Why do we struggle to fully surrender? We have been conditioned since birth to believe that it is not safe to be vulnerable, that it's not safe to let go. We have a hard-wired response to protect ourselves. Learned behaviour teaches us not to show weakness, to stay strong and to hold ourselves together no matter what.

What happens when we don't surrender? We hold onto so much in our body – our emotions, our traumas. We hold onto it all. This 'holding on' in our body causes us physical problems over time. It shows up in our body as disease (dis-ease). When we can recognise that what is happening in our bodies is mainly symptoms of other things – unresolved traumas, unexpressed emotions, holding on too tight to life/situations – we can start to look at it with fresh eyes. It is only when we get to this point in our lives that we start to question whether there is another way to live. When we get to the stage where we want to start living more in harmony with ourselves, we can then delve into the art of allowing. This is the act of 'surrendering'.

Surrendering is not about giving up. It is not about thinking that you're failing. Surrendering is about fully allowing any possible outcome in any given situation – even the outcomes that you don't want! Surrendering involves moving your awareness down to your heart space, getting your mind out of the way and just being.

Learning to surrender:

- Place your hand on your heart space.
- Breathe a few deep breaths to really connect to this area.
- Say, either out loud or in your head, 'I allow any and every possible outcome in this particular situation. And so, it is.'
- Inhale deeply and fully exhale.

Doing this exercise consciously allows you to move your mind out of the way to allow the Divine to work through you and to deliver the best and highest possible outcome. The mantra to repeat is 'surrender, allow and trust'.

'*Surrender*' - surrender fully to the situation, just let go.

'*Allow*' - Allow any possibility or outcome. Allowing is being able to move your desires out of the way and into acceptance of what is.

'*Trust*' - Trust that the highest outcome for all will manifest.

This means that it's not hanging onto the old and what is or what you would like things to be. It is fully accepting the 'now' and surrendering to what may be, whatever that outcome.

As you progress along this path of surrendering, you will find that in certain situations it becomes easier. You will start to notice that you are able to let go of the need for a specific outcome in some scenarios. I find that surrendering is much easier in situations where you are not emotionally invested in the outcome! For example, getting ready for a first date and trying to surrender to whether you are going to meet the man or woman of your dreams. As soon as desire or our emotions come into play, the act of successfully surrendering takes us to a much greater level! It is much harder and requires a greater level of discipline when the stakes are increased. Just like in judo, or karate, you start learning basic moves with a practice partner and then, once your confidence grows, you move up a skill level and compete with more intricate nuances of the sport and against competitors who are actively seeking your trigger points and weak spots. This is why it is a step-by-step process. Start by surrendering to the easier stuff in life first, like surrendering to finding the perfect outfit in time for an event or a new place to live before your current house sells. Then, when you've mastered the first level, start to practise surrendering to situations that are harder for you to relinquish control, maybe surrendering to knowing that your business will grow and expand in exactly the right way and bring in the money you require to pay your bills. With enough practice, you will find that this becomes easier to do.

Chapter 25

Lord Maitreya

Greetings, my dear friends. It is an honour to be able to converse with you all. There is much I wish to share with you about the topic of this book – Divine Living. What does Divine Living mean to me? What does it mean from the perspective of an Ascended Master, you may ask yourselves? From my perspective, to live divinely is as simple as breathing. It is the act of taking one breath and then another. It requires no more effort than allowing your body to take that exhale and then an inhale – it is the breath of life. It is only when our minds get in the way that the act of divine living becomes complicated. It is at this point that a simple process becomes over-complicated, appears too difficult to attain and is completely unachievable. So, my advice to you, my dears, is to try to switch off the mind. Try to live from a place of simplicity, a place of trust and a place of surrender. Sometimes, the obvious viewpoint or way of being can be the best path. Don't overcomplicate things by thinking that life needs to be harder than it is. There is no need to struggle or strife. Life can, and should, be filled with joy and happiness and should flow with a sense of peace. People get in their own way by thinking that life should not be this easy, this simple, that divinity needs to be worked for and a heart full of peace should only know peace after it has known endless struggle. Enough with this torturous route. Enough with this desire to have to feel worthy before you can become an awakened soul. This awakened state is available to all – right now – with your next breath. It is that simple. End the struggle today and make that decision to just BE. No matter what. Let all of life flow through you and flow around you. Visualise yourself as part of that flow of eternal life. You are this source energy. You are perfect. Just as you are. No ifs, no buts. No 'when I've achieved x, y & z'. Now. You are perfect NOW. Right here, in this moment. Just breathe, I love you all.

You may have this desire that life should have more meaning, that there is more to life than your current existence. You have a desire for a purpose, for your life to be more than yourself, to mean something. Let me assure you that there is more to life than your current existence and at the same time, nothing more. There just is this present moment. No more and no less. The more you allow the present moment, the now, just to be, to witness the present moment as the perfection of life – just as it is – without the need to change it, to witness the miracle of life, the miracle of a breath, the more this takes away the desire, the need for your life to mean anything more than this. You are a miracle. Every breath that you take is pure perfection and a miracle in itself. Your life means something just by your existence. If you can live your life by following what brings you joy, live your life from a place of as purest love that you can find in each moment, your life will have immense meaning and tremendous purpose. There is no need for any more effort than this. This is the gift of abundance; to live in a state of awareness and peace, knowing, without a doubt, that all your needs will be met and allowing your heart to remain open in unconditional and pure love.

Chapter 26

The Welcome Committee

After making the decision that I was 'all in' and surrendering to my mission, regardless of the seasickness issue, I resolutely made my way back onto the boat the following morning. I sat, mouth clenched, and jaw locked in determination to be with the whales no matter what was thrown at me. The ocean was a lot rougher than the previous day, which did nothing to ease my anxiety levels. However, I was distracted by a magnificent display of two whales breaching out of the water again and again. We were all in awe. It was just magical and breathtaking watching this male and female whale in their courtship ritual, watching them throw themselves out of the water so nearly half of their bodies were exposed before crashing back down into the ocean. They did this in perfect union as they celebrated their courtship. It was like a dance, an unfolding of a love story. Nagwal shared that this display was also in celebration of me making the decision to get back on the boat again. The wave of gratitude that radiated from these whales for me was overwhelming. I felt so humbled.

When we were given the go-ahead to go swimming with them, I somehow managed to get myself into the water. The gentle and graceful sliding into the water was still a skill I hadn't mastered, but I half fell, half plopped off the boat and I was in! It was much more difficult swimming in the choppy water than it had been the day before, but I was determined to continue. The rough waves sap your energy, and it takes longer to travel the same distance, not to mention the poor visibility. When our swim guide stopped at the area, he considered the best for being with the whales, we bobbed on the surface, heads down, looking for a glimpse of the magnificent creatures. We were rewarded as the pair swam right underneath us. It was such a phenomenal and spell-binding sight I think I stopped breathing for a short time. To be so close to these amazing beings was such a privilege.

We swam with these whales for over half an hour, but it seemed like only an instant had passed before we were asked to get back onto the boat. Once back on board the boat, the familiar feeling of seasickness started to surface and again, I lost the contents of my stomach over the side of the boat. Amazingly, I was only sick this once. My presence on the boat was not as dramatic as the day before, which was a huge relief for me as well as the fellow passengers who had to witness me being ill for so many hours. And a bonus was that I even managed to get back into the ocean again to swim with this mating pair. Back on the boat, I tuned into these whales, and they shared with me how they saw and felt our energies as a group. They showed me, what they saw from their vantage point from down in the depths of the ocean. Looking up, surrounded by a deep throbbing royal blue was a pink blob of heart-centred energy, our group! This pink ball was floating on the surface, and they also showed me an image of our swim guide, to demonstrate visually how in tune he was with the whales and how much they respected him. The visual they showed me was energetic light travelling between the whales and the swim guide, encompassing them all. They referred to him as 'brother', which I found just beautiful.

The whales also shared that not all groups that came to swim with them had the same energy, some were more in their mind than their heart space. The whales wanted to show me how people's energies had changed as a whole compared to a few years ago. I don't recall what they said specifically, but the general summary is that people now carry a lot less emotional baggage than they did in past years, which I find reassuring. The whales shared that when people swam with them, the whales helped to balance and re-calibrate the swimmers' energies via the frequencies that the whales emit. They shared that when I was in the water with them, unbeknown to my conscious self, we were exchanging codes and frequencies which I would be taking back to the UK and distributing in the British waters.

I also received a powerful message regarding my seasickness. I needed to surrender to the ocean, fully let go and allow myself to be vulnerable. That really made a lot of sense to me. As humans, we live so much of our lives with the illusion that we are in control. In reality, we have very little control over anything. So, the following day, and every day thereafter, when I got onto the boat, I went into a state of allowing and fully surrendering to the ocean and whatever she required of me that day. I wasn't sick again for the remainder of the retreat.

Part Eight

JOY

Chapter 27

Joy

> *Joy does not simply happen to us.*
>
> *We have to choose joy,*
>
> *And keep choosing it every day.*
>
> — *Henri Nouwen*

One of the key components to living divinely is 'JOY'. Being in the emotion of joy connects you directly to your divinity. It is like a straight and direct connection. Following what brings you joy enables your heart to open more fully. What brings you joy will be different for each and every one of you. For some, it will be spending time with loved ones, for others, it will be that bliss of having time alone. Making time for doing things that bring you joy is essential. It is so easy to prioritise others' needs above your own and think that we have to sacrifice our needs to make others happy. It is so easy to believe that we need to always be 'in service' to be worthy of love, constantly proving our worth by putting others first, whether this is our partner, children, friends or family.

We also have a tendency to label ourselves as 'selfish' if we put our needs before others. This is NOT selfish. This is self-care. Putting others first all the time is so draining on our energy and unhealthy long-term. If we are operating from a position of lack, where our own battery is drained, in reality, we have nothing to give another. When we top-up our own energy first, when we give ourselves permission to do things for ourselves and to discover what brings us joy, we enable ourselves to charge our own batteries first and then we can come from a place of fullness and completeness. We can be of far more help to others when we come from this place.

So how do we start to find joy? Following our joy is a journey. It is finding, moment to moment, what brings us happiness or allows us to experience it. Initially, we may find joy by having to be in a state of doing – reading a book, going for a walk or having a lovely meal with friends, for example. Allow whatever lights you up and makes you feel alive and full of joy. Don't judge whether it is a big or small thing. This point is irrelevant. Allow yourself to do things that make you happy. Prioritise your own happiness. Give yourself permission to do things that put a smile on your face and make your heart sing. If you have a busy life and have a lot of demands on your time, carve out small pieces of time just for you. No matter how impossible it may appear, I assure you, the time exists for these experiences. Even just a few minutes of something that feels like a ray of sunshine on a cloudy day is a step in the right direction.

Honour the time you put aside just for yourself. Acknowledge that this is what you are doing. Own the fact that you are doing this for you – just for you. It will increase that inner joy of knowing that you are prioritising yourself. It may not make any sense to anyone else but that does not matter – you know what lights you up.

This is the first step in welcoming joy to your life. Allow yourself to experience what makes you happy. Fill yourself up first so that you can best support others in your life. The next step is discovering divine joy. True joy comes from a feeling inside of us, not something that is created externally. True joy comes from the 'being' state rather than the 'doing'. It is that transcendent infinite love. Pure joy is found by just being. It is that state of stillness, the breath between breaths where the essence of joy is found. This is where you truly know that you are connected to the Divine. When you can feel joy running through every cell of your body. There is no explanation needed. There are no words to describe it. You just know. You feel a contentment, a sense of peace, a sense of pure joy. This place of being is just bliss. To be able to radiate out into the world from this state is to be able to connect to All That Is. It is connecting to your true power. The oneness that resides within.

When learning to follow your joy, you will just touch on glimpses of this state of being. You will have brief moments when you touch breaths with this feeling of pure joy. It will then be like a drug; you will want to exist in this place more and more. For it is when you are in this place that everything makes sense. Everything else in life just drops away. Everything else suddenly seems irrelevant and meaningless. Being in this state of alignment and pure joy, there is nothing else that lives up to this.

Chapter 28

Melchizedek

So often we miss what is important. We value the wrong things in life. Our focus is on the big things – career, relationships, money. Whereas we can sometimes miss that this is not the priority. It is the small moments in life that are really important – that act of simply being, breathing, the smell of flowers, The feel of the rain on your face, the sun shining in the sky, being with a loved one... All these little things are what bring us real joy. When we can appreciate these small things in life and really value their importance, the bigger things start to slot into place. It is not that they are not important or have no value. It is just that they lose their priority. They do not give the sense of peace, joy or stillness that is required to be able to live in connection with the universe – to live divinely. Once we can shift our perspective and focus on the smaller things in life, everything starts to slot into place. Life begins to make sense. Your life takes on a new meaning. It is like you can relax into your life more, breathe more deeply, have more fun and have a lighter approach. People often gain this perspective just before they die and pass back to Spirit. It is in this moment of transition that they gain clarity. They recognise what was truly important as they look back on their life. They gain perspective on what a waste of time they had spent on really quite irrelevant stuff, endless worrying and focus on things that were really not that important. Wouldn't it be wonderful if that sense of clarity could be gained earlier in life? The 'ah ha' moment reached when something could still be done about it, where you still had time to make those key changes in your life. This is the fundamental principle of Divine Living. Living in connection with the Divine, with your true self, allows you to gain that reflection, that wisdom, that clarity whilst you still have the breaths left to enjoy the fruits of this. Living on this planet in a physical body is truly a wondrous experience. It is a joy to experience all the highs and lows that life has to offer. The love, the pain – the full spectrum of emotions – are all there for you to experience. When you are able to gain this change in perspective, you start not to get lost in these depths of emotions. You don't drown in them. You are able to ride the waves of these emotions with a new-found freedom and clarity, with an inner peace, with joy and with love. Allow me to guide you in this process. Allow me to assist in lighting your path on this journey. Know that you can achieve this. This state of being is within your grasp. Just breathe and follow your heart. You've got this.

Chapter 29

Mission Day

Being in the ocean with the humpback whales brought me so much joy. The physical efforts required to actually be with them were maybe not so joyous for me, but the 'being' in the water with them – pure joy. Those magical moments were when time seemed to stand still. Watching them swim next to me in all their majesty and sovereignty took my breath away every single day. To me, it was like my heart and theirs beat as one. That pure transcendent joy. I felt so connected to them and to myself, as well as to the Divine, in those moments.

I never forgot the gratitude that I felt that Nagwal had chosen me to complete this mission. I may have questioned his judgement (several times!), but I was always in awe of what I was getting to experience and do with these magnificent creatures. I was being given the opportunity to do something extraordinary and I never took that for granted. I followed my guidance from Nagwal and from the others that I interacted with, trusting them to see the bigger picture of what was in play. For my part, I got to experience the absolute joy of swimming with these humpback whales.

'Mission day' finally arrived. While getting ready, Nagwal kept on repeating 'holy trinity' to me over and over again. When I tuned into him, he showed me orcas, dolphins and humpback whales forming a triangle, i.e., the holy trinity, with myself and Nagwal in the centre. I was not given any further specifics, but I knew that it related to our mission of enabling the Divine Feminine and Masculine energies to flourish once again on Earth. He also shared that the last couple of days had been in preparation for today. He requested that as soon as I got into the water, I was to connect to him, the whales, the orcas and the dolphins simultaneously. It was to enact this holy trinity formation. I could feel him energetically start to move around my body in a kind of spiral dance, looking a bit like a DNA helix. He said he was awakening my kundalini energy in preparation for being in the ocean today. In Sanskrit, kundalini means 'coiled snake' and it is a term used to describe the creative power and energy of the universe. Kundalini energy is believed to lie dormant at the base of the spine until it is awakened. I could feel the energy inside me, moving up and down my spine like a snake uncoiling, as he worked on me.

Today we had the beautiful experience of swimming with a mother whale and her calf again. The calf was really close to us because he still had to come to the surface to breathe regularly, but before I could fully enjoy this experience, I had a mission to complete! So, once in the water, I tuned into the various beings, as instructed by Nagwal, and then centred myself and him in the middle of this connection. I then fully opened my energy and just allowed what needed to happen to happen. I find with this multidimensional work we can often get in the way by trying to 'figure out' exactly what is happening. I get told by my guides that my human brain just couldn't comprehend exactly what was going on. When I am called upon to carry out any spiritual work, I just open up my energy, let go and allow what is needed. It certainly gives me a lot less of a headache than trying to fully understand what is happening!

To me, it felt slightly anticlimactic, but Nagwal was delighted. All of this work and preparation and this was it? I think I expected fireworks or something really dramatic to happen! I could feel his victorious energy with me for the whole day, as well as the delight of the whales and dolphins. Nagwal did inform me that my work was not yet complete and that today was just another stepping-stone in our journey working together. I didn't get fireworks, but I did get the reward of swimming with mummy and baby again, which was just exquisite as they both swam a full circle around our group. Just breathtaking.

As we are on the topic of joy and how much joy and love I received from being with the whales, I thought it only right to share the not-so-joyous physical reality. The reality of being with the whales was, for me, not so easy and came with its own set of challenges. Trying to not be sick on the boat was just one such challenge. The main issue for me was actually getting to the whales. I categorised these daily challenges into three:

1. Getting into the water
2. Swimming to the whales
3. Getting back on board the boat

The first point may sound a little silly to some, to actually note as one of my challenges. As I soon realised, getting into the water was not a challenge to me... getting into the water when I actually wanted to... now that was a different matter! I am not the most coordinated, to say the least. Even on dry land, coordination and balance are a bit of an issue for me. So, put me in a small boat on a rough ocean and balance and coordination went out the window. Add fins to this mix and I think you're building up quite an accurate picture. The first challenge was to get to the edge of the boat. There were only a couple of steps to reach the edge, but it was the challenge of not going head-first over the side of the boat that I found difficult. I have to point out that none of my retreat buddies had this issue... they looked and acted like reincarnated mermaids! The side of the boat was a few inches thick and there was a gap of a couple of feet wide, which was the best place to enter the water. I would precariously sit in this gap and try to swing my uncoordinated legs (with fins attached) over the side of the boat while still hanging onto the side. The ultimate aim was to then gently lower myself into the water, creating as little splash and noise as possible. Yeah right! I think I managed that graceful 'twist and enter' twice in the whole two weeks. I was just grateful at that point to get into the ocean in one piece.

My next task was to focus on the direction my group was swimming in. I found that no matter how prepared or speedy I tried to be, I was always last off the boat. When the call came that we could get into the water, my mermaid buddies were off the boat in seconds. It was like watching rats jump off a sinking ship! So, I was always playing catch up when finally in the water, trying to make my way to wherever they were. I just determinedly put my head down and kept swimming until I finally reached the rest of the group. The positive aspect of being so focused on the current task at hand is that I had no mental energy left to worry about sharks. My entire focus was keeping my body moving through the water until I caught up with everyone else, whilst not looking at the shark fin that just glided past me!

The best bit for me was when I finally caught up with the group and I got to rest as we floated on the surface observing and being with the whales. Absolute bliss. Plus, it gave me a chance to get my breath back!

The final part of my mission was getting back on board the boat. When the call came that it was time to get back on board, our boat would start making its way towards us. Having our boat firmly in my sights, I set off swimming until I reached my goal. A ladder was lowered so that we could climb aboard. Again, I found this process quite challenging. With one arm I would grab hold of the ladder and cling on to it for all it was worth. While being battered against the side of the boat with the rough ocean conditions, I then had to carefully remove my fins and throw them on board the boat before climbing up the ladder. I found getting my fins on and off a real challenge as well as not letting them go while still in the ocean! The ocean had been quite rough for most of the days, and I tended to fall into the boat rather than make a graceful arrival, but at least I was back on board.

I had a mantra that helped me get through each day in the ocean when I was being pushed way outside of my comfort zone. To help me stay motivated, I turned to one of the great spiritual gurus of our generation: Disney Pixar's, Finding Nemo! For those of you who have watched this amazing film, you will be able to understand the context to which I refer. For those who haven't, I would fully recommend watching the film if you get the opportunity. So, the mantra that I had on repeat in my head for those two weeks was the phrase:

'Just keep swimming!'

This was not the whimsical, upbeat phrase used by Dory to help when life got you down. No, this was the phrase used by Marlon at that point in the film where they were about to embark on scary adventures unknown. It was his gritty determination that was the motivating voice in my head.

You going in there? 'YEP!'

What you gonna do? 'JUST... KEEP... SWIMMING'

Part Nine

IT'S OKAY

Chapter 30

It's Okay

> *It's okay not to be okay all the time.*
>
> *Some days are just harder than others.*
>
> *Go through what you are going through and go with the flow.*
>
> — *(Unknown)*

It's OKAY that you think you're just not getting it, and that you're not getting it right. It's OKAY to think that you're failing and that other people seem just to naturally flow on their spiritual path. It's OKAY if you think you're doing it all wrong and you're just a messy heap on the floor. I assure you that you are doing perfectly. It's a journey. There is no right or wrong path, there just is. Just trust in your path. Know that there will be ups and downs. Know that everyone has bad days. It's not just you. Everyone has days when they are just sobbing their heart out thinking that they can't possibly take another step forward, that they don't know which direction to go in. Everyone thinks like that at some point in their life (or several points, if they're being totally honest). Just breathe. Know that tomorrow is a new day. You don't have to have it all figured out right now. Just hand it over to the Divine. Ask for higher guidance and then just let it go. It doesn't mean that things are instantly going to get better or you're going to have a neon sign suddenly light up and show you the way. No. It just helps knowing that you're not on your own. You don't have to figure it all out on your own. I think of it as delegating. You're just delegating to a higher power – the Divine. Their timing may not be the same as we would want but just by handing things over, you're sharing the problem and easing the burden. Doesn't that sound much lighter?

Just know that it's okay not to be okay. It's okay not to have all the answers. It's okay to not have it all figured out. It's okay if some days you can hardly get out of bed, or all you want to do is cry, or all that you *can* do is cry! It's okay. Some days are going to be like that, and it is about being gentle with yourself and recognising the fact that some days are just not going to be okay, and it is about getting through it as best as you can, and not being all holy and spiritual and feeling that you have to figure it all out and be all Zen. Some days are not going to be like that. Some days, you're going to be dragging yourself through the day by your fingertips and feeling like crap. And there are going to be days like that for whatever reason. Either stuff that is going on in your life or energies that are happening – intense portals or planetary changes are all going to affect and influence your energy and it will affect your mood and how you feel. And sometimes, bad things are going to happen. Sometimes, you're going to go through tough periods and that is part of what we signed up for. Know that it's not going to be all unicorns, fairies and rainbows all the time. It's wonderful when those times come but this is not how it is going to be all the time.

There are going to be ups and downs and just know that it is okay. You will get through it. Just recognising that it is a bad day and allowing yourself to flow with it helps you surrender to it. Give yourself permission to feel how you are feeling in that moment. It is about honouring your true feelings and not trying to pretend that everything is okay. Plastering a smile on your face and pretending that everything is 'love and light' when all you want to do is scream and shout is not truly honouring yourself. Allow yourself to scream and shout. Allow yourself to be angry. Allow yourself to cry. Allow yourself to be whatever you need to be.

Know that it is okay to not be okay. Give yourself that gift. Tomorrow, as they say, is another day. Tomorrow, you have another opportunity to feel better than you do today.

Chapter 31

Metatron

If I could offer one piece of advice to you it would be patience. Have patience with yourself. Trying to live in connection with your true essence takes practice. It is not something that you can master straight away without falling into any pitfalls. You have been living your life thus far in a particular way. You have been living predominantly from a mental space, a head space. To live in conjunction with the Divine requires you to live predominantly from the heart space, from the space of love. It takes time for this to become your default setting. It is achievable. Many have achieved it that have passed before you. Many are achieving it right now. But I suggest just breathing, taking your time. There is no rush. If you slip up and feel that you have failed in a particular moment, just breathe and try and make a different choice in the next moment. It requires practice to be able to fully embody a new way of being.

There is much going on on your planet right now. Now is the time to be gentle with yourself and really practise self-care. The energies on your planet are very much in flux. There is a steady increase in the vibration of the energy on planet Earth and everything that resides on her. This increase in vibration takes its toll on your energetic and physical body. You are constantly readjusting to these changing frequencies as planet Earth is moving from a third-dimensional frequency into a fully fifth-dimensional frequency. The result of this is that your physical body will be living in a multi-dimensional reality. Many different timelines will be available to you, and it will take a while to adjust to living in this new way. Part of what will ease this adjustment is the new way of being, living in flow and harmony with your true essence. Your soul has lived previously in these higher multi-dimensional frequencies. It knows how to traverse these frequencies with ease. It is a case of remembering, of allowing this remembering to occur. For this 'remembering' to occur it requires the first step to come from a cognitive place - a decision to want to choose a different way of being to the current one that you are in, a desire to act, to live, to be different in each and every moment. Renew this desire with each and every breath and with each and every step. The renewing of this desire will eventually become automatic. This different state of being will be fully remembered. You will now be living your life consciously from a place of love, expansiveness and completeness. This does not mean to say that you no longer go through human trials while you are in this incarnation. It does not mean that you live your life with no bumps in the road. Living in harmony with the universe gives you a totally different perspective of these incidents. It allows you to have a deeper understanding of your life and also life on Earth in its totality. To operate from this space of grace and peace is a state of being, not a state of thinking. Are you willing to commit to changing your focus and having your life forever changed? We are here to guide you on this journey. Know that you are fully supported and allow us to light the way.

Chapter 32

The Day I Was Not Okay

On this particular day, we had the morning free to explore the island before setting out on the boat in the afternoon. Moorea is closely connected to the energies of Avalon and the Egyptian pyramids, so the energy on the island was really powerful. The sacred sites were located in the middle of the island and the tropical rainforest landscape was a complete contrast to the teal-blue ocean shores that I was now familiar with. It was a very humid and damp environment, which naturally attracted a large population of mosquitoes. The energy around these sites felt very sacred, ancient and reverent. We spoke in hushed whispers. I felt the trees and land downloading codes and information into me, and I was told that the others in our group were receiving similar. We were to take these codes with us that afternoon to the ocean and the whales.

From the moment we boarded the boat that afternoon, I can only describe the energy as frenetic and chaotic. To start with, we boarded to the news that the boat had nearly sunk that morning. The motor on the boat was struggling initially which did not fill me with confidence. The whole afternoon was really surreal and bizarre. The ocean was really rough, with the waves increasing in size the further we went out. Due to these large waves, the boat kept taking on water which the captain frantically bailed out with a bucket! Not a comforting sight to witness!

When we came across a whale, the normal calm routine of entering into the water went totally out the window. Our normally very placid captain started yelling - to this day I still don't know who or what he was yelling at - but it sent me into a frenzied panic thinking he was yelling at me, so I went overboard into the water with an even louder splash than usual. The ocean was really rough, the roughest that we had swam in. I just focused on where we were heading with grim determination, my 'just keep swimming' mantra circling in my head. The swim went on for ages, and we must have covered nearly a mile in distance. To make matters worse, the whales had vanished by the time we got close, so we got straight back onto the boat. I was physically exhausted but pleased that I had managed to swim such a distance.

The next whale sighting and drop-point for us swimmers was only a short while afterwards and, again, it was a really long swim. With the water being so rough, it just sapped the energy out of me making the swim even more difficult and strenuous. It felt like an uphill battle, the muscles in my arms and legs were screaming for respite. Being the slowest swimmer, I did my best to keep an eye on at least one group member, however with the waves being so big I kept losing sight of the second-last swimmer, so it was as if I was just swimming out in the middle of the ocean on my own. When I totally lost sight of her, I'd reached a point where my body just screamed 'ENOUGH!' at me. I physically had no energy left to swim another stroke. I couldn't see where anyone else was, and all I could see were very large waves everywhere. I can comprehend now that my next reaction wouldn't be considered normal: a 'normal' reaction would probably have been a meltdown of some sort, a panic attack maybe from the stark realisation that I was in a very dire situation - the normal survival instincts kicking in. No, my reaction was to very calmly state that I had enough, I am not swimming anymore... and sharks, you can come and get me now! (not my finest moment!) and I just let go.

In the next second, I felt Nagwal come charging into my energy field like a tornado and I was hit with his words 'NOT ON MY WATCH!' I was too far gone at this point to answer him back. I had no concept of time as I peacefully started to sink, but in what seemed a really short space of time, our swim guide suddenly surfaced right in front of me, grabbed me and started to pull me along with him. I dimly recollect that he pulled me for quite a while, which showed the distance that I had been separated from the others and then he continued pulling me until I reached the safety of the boat. I was still quite spaced out but extremely grateful for his intervention. Getting back on the boat caused me a bit of drama. With the water being so rough, I was pummelled against the side of the boat as I held onto the ladder trying to get my fins off. Combined with complete exhaustion, this process seemed to take forever. Even trying to get up the ladder and back onto the boat was challenging for me, I literally had no energy left. I remember reaching the top of the ladder and just falling into the boat. I was so traumatised at this point and my physical body was in so much pain that I just lay down on the boat and energetically left my body. I had no real recollection of the remainder of the trip. I was off floating in the cosmos and not wanting to really connect back with my battered and bruised body. During the swim and getting back on the boat I had hurt my shoulder and neck as well as being bruised down one side of my body, so I was in quite a bit of physical pain, not to mention the emotional distress!

Afterwards, on dry land, while talking to another retreat member, I put together some of the missing pieces. Apparently, the rest of the group were all together in the water looking for the whales. Then, without warning and not saying a word, the swim guide dived underwater and swam off leaving them all. I think, at this point, our swim guide had been hit by a cosmic blast from Nagwal of 'Go save Kirstie!' I am so grateful to him and Nagwal for saving me. Clearly, Nagwal had more work for me to do (including writing this book!) so dying at this point was not on his game plan!

I made the decision not to go onto the boat the following day. I had to actually acknowledge that I was not okay and give myself permission to just be; to have time and space away from the group and process what had happened and to process my emotions, give my body an opportunity to heal and to rest. And that was okay. It was part of learning to prioritise myself and have a much-needed time out.

I took the opportunity to reach out to Nagwal to gain some perspective on the previous day. He said that the long swims had been necessary as we were dropping the energetic codes and frequencies into the water that had been collected from the sacred sites that morning. They were required to be anchored in over a large distance. The chaotic energy that I sensed that afternoon facilitated this process.

Part Ten

DIVINE UNION

Chapter 33

Divine Union

> *The heart of the matter is always our oneness with divine spirit, our union with all life.*
>
> — Nhat Hanh

Divine union is when two halves of a whole are united. It is when a perfect balance of masculine and feminine energies comes together to form a perfect whole. The two fit together like a DNA strand, a helix of perfect divine balance. Divine union happens initially within an individual where they weave together the perfect balance of masculine and feminine energy within themselves. The second happens between two separate people meeting to form a perfect, balanced partnership. Some may refer to this as soul mates or twin flames.

Within a person, there are both masculine and feminine energies. This has nothing to do with gender. Masculine and feminine energies are just that – energies. These energies have particular traits. The masculine energy is a 'doing' energy, it is an active energy. The masculine energy is very much about planning, strategy and activity. It is a direct energy that is about completing tasks and getting things done. Feminine energy is more about being in flow. It is a 'being' energy. It is about wisdom and intuition. It has a more cyclic nature to it, such as living in harmony with the moon and her cycles.

For centuries, we as a society have been living out of balance. We have been dominated by the masculine energy. We have been existing in what would be referred to as a patriarchal society. This is where the dominant focus has been on 'doing'. The focus has been on career, money, achieving and strategising. The art of listening to your intuition and flowing more with the cycles of mother nature has been suppressed, forgotten and consequently, not valued. Recently in the past few years, this feminine energy has started to be remembered again. Some refer to this as a rise of the Divine Feminine. There has been much movement in the rising of this energy and the remembering of an old way of being. Some think that this is occurring to overpower the masculine-dominated society, for life to become dominated by the feminine. No. This is not the case. It is about bringing back the balance between the masculine and feminine energy so that they exist in perfect union and harmony with each other. Both energies are required to create perfect balance - the balance between the being and the doing. The feminine energy of connecting to inner wisdom and knowing combined with the masculine of acting on that inspiration. If we swing completely to the feminine energy and live in that 'being' energy not a lot would get done. We require the masculine energy to carry out tasks, but they need to be centred around an intuitive flow rather than a structured checklist.

Initially, a person needs to balance their own masculine and feminine energies within themselves. Again, this has nothing to do with gender. This in itself is referred to as a Divine Union. The perfect balance of Divine Feminine and Divine Masculine energy. Divine Union also exists outside a person, when two people come together that are both in perfect balance and create two halves of a whole. These relationships are based on harmony and balance. In a divine union, the two souls have undergone their own personal healing, so they are not looking for the other person to 'save' them. There is the absence of any neediness or rescuing energy which is the basis for a lot of relationships. The majority of relationships are based on co-dependency of some sort to a greater or lesser extent where they each fulfil a need in the other. A Divine Union relationship is based on perfect balance, where each party is whole and requires nothing from the other apart from being together with love.

The world has become out of balance with these energies, and we are now being asked to bring it back into balance. We need both energies within us, in perfect balance, to allow ourselves to embrace our divinity and to be part of this ascending New Earth. Aligning with our true self creates the energetic frequencies of the Divine Feminine and Divine Masculine. These energies are only just returning to our planet. The Divine Feminine has to be embodied and remembered first. This then allows the Divine Masculine energy to be awakened as this energy needs to be 'birthed' through the Divine Feminine. The Divine Feminine is the creation energy, the womb space for the Divine Masculine to be birthed again.

There are currently many Divine Feminine and Divine Masculine beings that are helping us to achieve this balance (some have channelled chapters in this book). Beings that have walked this earth in previous incarnations are stepping forward to guide us on this journey and help us to remember a long-forgotten way of living, encouraging us to allow our feminine energy to rise, to take her place in perfect balance with the masculine energy. These Divine

Feminine and Masculine beings are providing a blueprint for us to remember what the divine energies feel like. The Divine Feminine is about stepping into our power, holding space and valuing ourselves and our intuition. The Divine Masculine energy is about clear communication, being anchored and connected to our emotions.

The current masculine and feminine energies present themselves as what is often referred to as wounded or distorted. This means that they are not displaying the true qualities or frequency of the divine energies. These wounded energetic traits can be seen in both the masculine and feminine. The wounded or distorted masculine energy can be seen as the inability to be emotionally present, numbing with addictions, fear of being vulnerable and being controlling or domineering. The wounded feminine energy can be seen as disengaged from the self, feeling of being powerless, having no voice and not being visible.

In order for us to fully embody our divinity, we need to be able to face our shadow, the darkness that resides within all of us. There can be no light without the dark, therefore, to fully embody our light we must be prepared to accept our darkness too. This is often referred to as shadow work. There are feminine beings that are assisting us in this process who are referred to as the Dark Divine Feminine (such as Lilith and Mary Magdalene, for example). These beings are lovingly assisting us to allow all parts of ourselves to be seen and acknowledged. For centuries we have been encouraged to display only the 'good' parts of ourselves – the good girl, the good boy, the people pleaser, the demure exterior. We have been conditioned that it is not acceptable to speak up, to display emotions such as anger or jealousy as these are perceived as negative or 'bad'. It was considered not acceptable to have judgments or to have outbursts. These emotions and traits have been suppressed. It is time now to allow them to the surface. To know that it is okay to express your anger, your sexual feelings, your jealousy or your judgments for instance. There is no shame in these. We have been conditioned to feel shame surrounding these emotions and feelings. No more. Allow them to rise to the surface and to be acknowledged. It is only when we can face our darkness that we can start to fully embrace our light.

Chapter 34

Mary Magdalene

My dearest brothers and sisters, it brings me deep joy to be here with you. It is an honour to be able to discuss my thoughts and views on what it means to live in connection with the Divine. To me, being able to connect to your divinity is about balance. It is about achieving a balance within your life both externally and internally i.e., both within and without, to have complete balance between all parts of yourself and in all parts of your life. Connecting to the Divine can be only achieved with harmony. The state of alignment, of union, can only happen when there is perfect balance, the balance between the masculine and feminine energies, both within and without. These two energies are the perfect partnership, the yin and yang of each other. One complements the other perfectly. Divine union is the joining of the two aspects of the soul. The intuitive energy is completely anchored and held within the supportive framework - the picture of complete balance, the absence of competition or strife. Each part of the whole is no more or less than the other. Both parts work in peace, harmony and love. The intertwining of these two aspects is pure divine union. It is when this is achieved, that this complete surrender to the universe occurs. An acceptance of what is and what will be. The previous resistance that is held within yourself and towards life itself just melts away. A wider perspective and understanding are gained of how everything in your life weaves together in divine union and divine timing. It is at this point that a sense of peace washes over you. The aspects of your life that previously seemed important lose their priority. You gain clarity and a higher understanding of what is important. The focus shifts from external things in your life to your internal happiness. That happiness and joy that come from within is unshakable. It is like a pillar of light in the darkness. It is your strength; it is where your power is, in that space of nothingness within, in the void deep within. This is where all the answers lie. It is deep within that void that the union of the parts of yourself is discovered. It is the perfect weaving of the intuitive and active parts of yourself, by allowing yourself to listen to the intuitive whispers that are only heard within the silence. Allow these beautiful drops of inspiration to propel the action, to be the rudder for the forward impulsion.

It is when these two halves of yourself are reunited and start operating in complete balance with each other that you can truly connect to your divinity. This union occurs within when you start to embrace all parts of yourself, without judgement. When you forgive yourself and others for all perceived wrongs in life and you start to surrender and allow us, the Divine, to work through you for your highest good and the highest good of all. It is when this state of surrender and allowing is fully present within your life that this state of alignment is achieved. This state of alignment can be achieved in just one breath. It is that simple. However, it usually takes many breaths to achieve as it remains elusive as to how simple a process it is. It requires the suspension of all the old conditionings, all the old constructs and paradigms and this takes a certain number of breaths, depending on the individual. There is no right or wrong in how many breaths this takes. There just is. Allow yourself to fully connect to this process today. Allow yourself to embark on this journey. To start to go within and to discover those missing pieces of yourself that have remained dormant. Make this commitment to yourself today, in this moment, in this now. Blessed be.

Chapter 35

The Ultimate Balance

My final week with the whales was for me to work on balancing the masculine and feminine energies on the planet, along with Nagwal. I was advised that I would be bringing cosmic energy down through me and, with the assistance of the whales, connecting these energies to the Earth. I was told that this would allow fear from the collective to come up and be balanced again with the feminine and masculine energies.

I got to experience these various energies being balanced and cleared in different ways during that week. I witnessed the depth of the healing work that the whales facilitated. I finally understood why I was required to undergo so much healing and releasing, prior to my being with the whales. Whales have the ability to trigger deep emotions within you, that you potentially didn't even know that you were carrying, to facilitate deep cellular healing. As I was technically 'working' with them it was considered helpful that my healing needs didn't interfere with the work we were doing – hence the need for me to clear a lot of my stuff prior to the trip. I was held in the eye of the storm, and I got to witness many others being triggered and offered opportunities to heal by the whales. I have so much gratitude for the whales and what they do for us as humans, as well as for the Earth herself.

It was getting difficult to ignore the constant dizziness that I was experiencing, even when not on the boat. My whole body and energy field were constantly in motion. A very helpful bird shared his wisdom with me while I was relaxing on my balcony one morning. He said life is about balance, balance between water and land, light and dark, feminine and masculine. It is about finding and navigating that point of balance. When I allowed myself to be in balance, I would no longer have that constant movement when on dry land. He was right. Once I had received the message and understood it, the dizziness vanished.

One of the highlights of the retreat for me was swimming with a mummy, her calf and a singer whale. This singer whale was acting as an escort for this whale and her calf. The frequency of the sound being emitted by this singer was phenomenal. I have never experienced anything like it – the melodious sound hitting my body, wave upon wave, causing my heart to expand with each wave. I could have stayed underwater listening to that song for eternity. I never wanted it to end. The vibration was completely heart-centered and when I returned to the boat, my heart space was so open I just had to let the tears roll down my cheeks in pure love and gratitude. Nagwal shared that the frequency was helping to clear the wounded masculine and feminine energies. Firstly, in the people that were in the ocean with the whale that day but also within the collective whole of the human species. Swimming with the baby whale was the most amazing experience. At one point, he swam right up close to me with his pectoral fins wide open exposing his whole underbelly and then locked eyes with me. I could have died happy right then. I was complete.

The whales shared with me how they honour the cycles of the moon and live in balance with nature. Balance between the feminine and masculine energies both within themselves and with each other. That perfect Divine Union. For example, they shared that they are much more active on the New Moon energies, whilst they are much less active during the Full Moon energies and allow themselves to just be. While they are working with people who come to swim with them, they are more in their masculine, holding the space to facilitate the healing. To balance this energy, they make sure they have time away from people to allow themselves to recharge. They shared that they use powerful energies such as portals, solstices and equinoxes to move into the feminine energy, be in receiving mode and allow their depleted energies to be restored. The retreat fell on the Autumn Equinox and the Full Moon and on both of these occasions, we did not see any whales. It was like they had gone to ground and just vanished. We could learn a lot from these beautiful creatures and how they honour themselves and their energies and live in perfect balance.

Part Eleven

CONCLUSION

Chapter 36

Final Words

Divine Living is not about being happy all the time. It is not about plastering a smile on your face and pretending everything is okay through gritted teeth. It requires you to be authentic. It is acknowledging your feelings – all of them – even the bad ones. It encourages you to put boundaries in place. It is letting go of control and surrendering to the universe and the Divine. It is understanding that there is a higher purpose and that ultimately, it will all be okay. It may not be in the form that you want things to work out, but it will be okay. It is about having that trust and that belief. It is deciding to embark on a journey of self-discovery – a journey of coming home to yourself. Allow yourself that gift, that freedom and that peace.

I am not saying that bad things won't happen to you. Life will continue to happen in and around you. Situations will continue to rise that will challenge you, day after day. You can decide to see these situations as challenges or opportunities. These situations give you the chance to choose how you respond. These opportunities show you how you have changed and healed when you respond differently from your normal default. They also bring clarity to where you still respond in the same way, giving you the choice to focus on these recurring patterns. It is about seeing life as an adventure and being willing to let go and allow it to take you to places that you could never have dreamed possible. Let us all take that leap of faith and start walking through life with fear, as a friend. Allow ourselves to surrender, spread our wings and fly.

For me, my journey with the Divine continues to unfold as I follow my guidance. I practise the teachings in this book daily as I continue to heal and endeavour to embody my true self and embrace my divinity. I live in a state of trust and surrender and allow my guidance to take me on whatever path is divine will. On my return from Tahiti, I had a beautiful, powerful lion come forward telling me to, you guessed it, 'come find me'. He advised that we would be working on the Christ Consciousness together. So, South Africa is calling me for my next big mission with the Divine. In 2023, I will be heading off to be with him. His name is Braveheart.

Chapter 37

Closing by Nagwal

Dearest brothers and sisters, it is with deep gratitude and thanks that I write these words to you. It is my humblest intention that you have read the words in this book and have taken away whatever resonates with you. Allow the words, the teachings and the message to wash over you. Allow the codes that have been embedded in this narrative to be downloaded into your cells, into your DNA, to allow a remembering to occur when you are ready to receive this message. This message, this remembering of your own sovereignty, your own Christ Consciousness, your own Divine Feminine and Divine Masculine energies resides within each and every one of you. For some, these cells have started to awaken. For others, the process is just beginning. Allow yourself to be with wherever you are on your journey. You are all perfect and are exactly where you are meant to be.

It has been an inspiring journey for me to be able to witness and observe my beautiful sister and fellow cosmic being, Kirstie. We have travelled many times together and in many forms, and I never cease to be amazed at the depths to which she can go. I hope the courage that it took to accomplish the tasks that I asked of her comes across clearly in her words. Her unwavering faith in me and the Divine is received with so much love and gratitude. We will travel together for some time as we continue to weave together a Divine Union in all forms of life on Earth.

I want you to know, dearest brothers and sisters, that I travel with you ALL and am helping each and every one of you to remember the magnificent sovereign beings that you are.

Chapter 38

Glossary of Ascended Masters and Goddesses

Isis - is a powerful Egyptian goddess of life, magic and healing. Known as the 'Goddess of Ten Thousand Names', she holds the magic power of so many other deities. Her husband was Osiris and her son, Horus.

Kal**i** - is a Hindu goddess, carrying the energy of both destruction and creation of life and the universe. She is a symbol of Shakti, the feminine creative energy and represents transformation, empowerment and spiritual liberation.

Lilith - is known in Jewish mythology as biblical Adam's first wife. She embodies the sexual energy of the Divine Feminine and is a deep, transformative force of the feminine spirit.

Lord Maitreya - is often referred to in Buddhism as the Future Buddha and is the embodiment of loving kindness. He is the keeper of the Cosmic Christ and represents enlightenment, wisdom, compassion and ascension.

Mary Magdalene - also known as Mary of Bethany was a key disciple in Jesus's ministry and witness to his crucifixion and resurrection. She represents the sacred Divine Feminine energies. She oversees the Divine Flame and Sacred Union of the masculine and feminine.

Melchizedek - is a great spiritual master of alchemy and sacred geometry. He is an ancient cosmic being in charge of the Order of Melchizedek, which is focused on the integration of Christ consciousness into all of humanity.

Metatron - is a powerful archangel of immense spiritual fire, wisdom and divine light. He holds the crystalline sacred geometry template of both the matrix and the awakened earth. He is actively involved in overseeing humanity's ascension.

Nagwal - a powerful cosmic being that chose to incarnate in 2015 as a humpback whale to assist in the ascension of Gaia and all of humanity.

Quan Yin - is the Buddhist goddess of compassion, mercy and healing. In Sanskrit, her name means 'Born of the Lotus'. She represents unconditional love and possesses the power to ease suffering and comfort those in need.

Yeshua - also known as Jesus, is the central figure in Christianity. He was a living example of the Christ Consciousness and guides us to embrace our own divinity. He teaches unconditional love, joy, forgiveness and devotion to the Christ within.

CHAPTER 39

ABOUT THE AUTHOR

Kirstie Lilith is a divine channel and animal communicator, committed to helping individuals and animals discover their voice. Her passion lies in guiding souls towards a profound connection with their authentic selves, embracing the divine masculine and feminine aspects that await reawakening.

Drawing upon her unique abilities, Kirstie channels the wisdom of the Ascended Masters and Goddesses to provide clarity and calmness during transformative life moments. She firmly believes that we are all destined to evolve into the highest version of ourselves.

With extensive experience in various energy practices, Kirstie works internationally, offering mentorship, training, retreats and private sessions. Her unwavering dedication centres around facilitating spiritual awakenings and supporting others on their journey of self-discovery.

Kirstie extends her transformative services through group programs and personalised one-on-one sessions.

You can find Kirstie online at the following link:

www.kirstielilith.com

Printed in Great Britain
by Amazon

37809295R00116